# WHAT GOOD IS GOD?

# WHAT GOOD IS GOD?

## CRISES, FAITH, AND RESILIENCE

### EDITED BY
### REVD DR ROGER ABBOTT
### PROFESSOR ROBERT WHITE

MONARCH
BOOKS

Published by
**Lion Hudson Limited**
Wilkinson House, Jordan Hill Business Park
Banbury Road, Oxford OX2 8DR, England
www.lionhudson.com

ISBN 978 0 85721 965 7
e-ISBN 978 0 85721 966 4

First edition 2020

### Acknowledgments

Every effort has been made to trace copyright holders and to obtain permission for the use of copyright material. The publisher apologizes for any errors or omissions and would be grateful to be notified of any corrections that should be incorporated in future reprints of this book.

Unless otherwise stated, Scripture quotations are taken from The New Revised Standard Version of the Bible copyright © 1989 by the Division of Christian Education of the National Council of Churches in the USA. Used by permission. All rights reserved.

Scripture quotations marked ESV are taken from The Holy Bible, English Standard Version® (ESV®) copyright © 2001 by Crossway, a publishing ministry of Good News Publishers. All rights reserved.

Scripture quotations marked *The Message* are taken from *The Message*. Copyright © by Eugene H. Peterson 1993, 1994, 1995, 1996, 2000, 2001, 2002. Used by permission of NavPress Publishing Group.

Scripture quotations marked NIV are taken from the Holy Bible, New International Version Anglicised, Copyright © 1979, 1984, 2011 Biblica, formerly International Bible Society. Used by permission of Hodder & Stoughton Publishers, an Hachette UK company. All rights reserved. "NIV" is a registered trademark of Biblica.

A catalogue record for this book is available from the British Library

Cover picture: The ruins of the National Cathedral in Port-au-Prince, Haiti, following the devastating earthquake of 12 January 2010. (Source: UNESCO, CC BY-SA 3.0 IGO)

Printed and bound in Great Britain by Clays Ltd, Elcograf S.p.A.

We dedicate this book to all those who, through their survival of or response to disasters, are committed to disaster response and mitigation by seeking to hold the needs of the survivors and deceased as their primary focus, and who are also dedicated to the systemic and structural changes that are necessary for this commitment to be more effective and just. We also dedicate the book in remembrance of those who have lost their lives or their livelihoods through disasters and from whom essential lessons have still to be learned and implemented. We dedicate the book in defiance of those whose ambitions are to turn occasions of disaster into their own financial and/or political benefit.

# CONTENTS

# ACKNOWLEDGMENTS

The editors would like to acknowledge their indebtedness to all those who participated in the workshop run by The Faraday Institute for Science and Religion, held at Westminster College, Cambridge, in April 2018, which was the inspiration for this book. We are also indebted to the Templeton World Charity Foundation for their funding of that workshop. We want to thank each of those who have contributed chapters and Lion Hudson for agreeing to publish the contributions in this edited book form. We thank Jon Oliver, Senior Commissioning Editor for Lion Hudson, for guiding us along the publishing route and for reminding us of important deadlines, but also for his understanding and flexibility in the process. Finally, we acknowledge our indebtedness to those around the world who have suffered the impacts of disasters, and who have shared their experiences as learning opportunities with us, in the hopes and prayers that changes will be made to ensure fewer lives are lost and life-changing injuries incurred when disasters strike in the future, as, during the duration of this "fallen" world, they inevitably will.

# INTRODUCTION

This is an inspired book! That is not intended as a pretentious claim. We do not mean it in the way we might talk about the Bible; we would not claim this book as being "God-breathed", as the Apostle Paul affirmed to be true, at very least, of the Old Testament Scriptures to his younger colleague Timothy (2 Timothy 3:16). The book you are reading is inspired by the passionate interest shown by those who participated in a workshop, run by The Faraday Institute for Science and Religion, under the heading of "Disasters, Faith, and Resilience" at Westminster College, Cambridge, in April 2018.

We designed the workshop to bring together participants who were academics and responders to disasters, but also to include the most significant contributors for such a workshop, who in our view are those who have experienced and survived disasters. Our feeling was that the requirement to listen before learning is an essential principle, and that *listening to survivors* is the most essential ingredient of that principle. All too frequently, the voices of survivors have been contained only in the stories they have been asked to publish for a readership perhaps more interested in being entertained than educated, and emotionally moved more than cognitively challenged. It is our conviction that survivors of disasters are significant knowledge and wisdom providers when it comes to how best to construct programmes for disaster response and mitigation. We buck the trend of assuming that survivors are mentally hamstrung, weak, inert, passive beings who require things being done for them or who need to be told what to do. In fact, it is our experience that they are incredibly strong, motivated, and intelligent sources for disaster education, deserving of empowerment, and capable of responsibility. Thus, we feel hugely privileged that our "survivors" responded enthusiastically to our invitation to join us for the workshop and to contribute chapters to this book.

It might be thought that sitting comfortably on our own turf in a Cambridge College gives us no right to pontificate on disasters. But among us were people who out of the blue had experienced almost unimaginable dislocation and suffering: one whose daughter had been killed in a terrorist attack only hours after saying goodbye following a pre-Christmas family gathering; another who had witnessed their home and their country torn apart by a devastating earthquake in Haiti, with hundreds of dead and dying around them; a third who had been ministering to Ebola victims only to see their close medical colleague struck down by the same disease and only in the nick of time brought back from the brink of death; another who had experienced the anguish of buildings, homes, and communities torn apart by the Hurricane Katrina flooding. They brought tears to our eyes but also a deep sense of our shared humanity, and of gratitude for the work of so many nameless volunteers and helpers who put their own needs aside to care for others. Though it looks as if we are comfortable and secure, in fact disaster and tragedy can strike at any time – even right in our own homes – as it did for John Mosey in the Lockerbie terrorist bombing. None of us is immune, although as ever it is the poor and the disadvantaged of whatever society who are hit hardest whatever the disaster.

At the conclusion of the workshop there was a serious desire conveyed by participants to the organizers that what had been heard from the keynote speakers, and from the attendant question-and-answer discussions, must not be "kicked into the long grass", as we say. What we had shared in together and learned must not be consigned to the history of too many workshops or to academic institutions' backroom library archives. There was a demand for something to emerge that would ensure the debates continued and, more significantly, that theological and scientific thinking on, and ethical practices in, disaster response would change the status quo. This participant desire chimed greatly with one of our key mission principles at The Faraday Institute, namely the need to disseminate our research learning. In other words, this book is *participant* inspired. We, the editors, can only hope that what you, the reader, are about to engage with will fulfil the desires of those who participated in the workshop, and that you will understand why they so desired to keep the discussions going.

The views expressed in the following chapters are those of the respective authors. As editors, we have felt it has been our role to solicit the submissions, not to control the substance of those submissions, and then to place them into an order that best serves, in our view, the overall purpose of the book.

Setting an appropriate order for the chapters has not been an easy task. Initially, we thought that hearing from the voices of the survivors first would be the best place to start, since it is their voices that too often are not captured, that go unheard, or get drowned beneath academic theories or organizations' and practitioners' inflexible policies. For the book to be most useful, however, we have chosen to place those survivors' voices at the heart of the book, not as bookends, so to speak.

What follows in the next chapters, starts, therefore, with a mix of theological, historical, and narrative reflections on disasters from Robert White, Jonathan Moo, and Roger Abbott to provide a general lens through which to look at disastrous incidents. Then comes Linda Mobula's description of her role as a medical academic and as a responder–practitioner, helping to extend the bridge between theological and historical reflection and the actual scenarios and experiences of disasters. She leads us into the heart of the book, namely to the chapters containing the personal narratives of four survivor accounts of catastrophic disasters, and their personal reflections on different aspects of disasters: John Mosey, Marie and Lucie, Luc Honorat, and Ken Taylor. Finally, comes an invited chapter from Hugh Rollinson on the climate crisis, the single issue that threatens to ensure that the occurrence of major disasters, such as those related in the prior chapters of this book, is going to increase for the coming generations.

## A closer look at the chapters ahead

White's chapter focuses upon the historical evidence of disasters. He moves the attribution of blame for disasters away from God, and away from the good and serviceable creation God created, to ourselves as responsible – or, more accurately, as irresponsible – human beings. The dysfunctional ways in which we handle the creation renege upon the divine mandate for us to steward the creation for the sake of others and to please God the Creator. Drawing on both historical and geophysical data from disasters involving earthquakes, volcanoes, floods, and climate change, and with his additional use of theology as commentary, White makes a compelling case for human culpability in the mismanagement of creation, and especially in the way natural *hazards* can turn disastrous.

Moo then explores how disasters are portrayed in the Bible, giving us a "30,000 ft" altitude perspective on disasters as seen from the viewpoint of the Scriptures. Referencing some of the early church fathers, he establishes a case for natural hazards being a necessary good arising out of the goodness of God as Creator. In particular, he reflects upon the biblical sense of viewing disasters as forms of *apocalypse*, not in the contemporary media fascination with that word as catastrophic drama (though there can be enough of that in disasters without the media's cashing in on it), but understanding *apocalypse* to mean a revealing or unveiling of both God's power and of human limitations. Moo reminds us that our response to the threat of disasters is to emulate that of God in Jesus Christ through lament, humility, saving life, and giving hope, with an additional important focus on our part, namely on repentance.

Abbott continues the theological case as well as introducing survivors' testimonies, taken from his interviews of disaster survivors in their localities, with his chapter focusing upon God's ontological and beneficent goodness. He asks what God's goodness is, in respect to disasters. He reflects upon the divine ontology of goodness – the assertion that God has been, is, and will always be good; that goodness is rooted and measured by God's own inherent goodness. Abbott then explores the more practical claim of God's beneficent goodness: his usefulness, especially when it comes to addressing disasters. Some might argue that this is what lies at the root of their grievance with disasters and religion: that all too often it seems that God is no use in disasters. From his research into this issue, however, Abbott contends it is in what God *does* in response to disasters, as narrated by survivors, that becomes the greatest challenge to the secular perspective and to the critiques of the role of faith that are often the focus in more strictly academic theodicy studies.

Mobula's chapter extends the transition from theology and history to practice. She brings her experience in internal medicine and infectious disease control, as both a medical academic and a responder–practitioner, to bear on her experience in addressing both the cholera (Haiti) and Ebola (Africa) virus epidemics of recent years. In particular, she reflects upon the importance of how science and faith need to be significant constituents to disaster responses where disease is a key factor. She shares with us some of the challenges to faith she has encountered in her work as an Emergency Room hospital medic, and in particular when called to respond to contexts involving disasters and major contagious diseases in low-income countries, where high-risk clinical decisions are required within very short timescales and with limited clinical resources. She describes how vital a role her Christian faith has played in the seriously demanding disaster contexts of healthcare.

Taking us right to the heart of the book, to the narrative testimonies of actual survivors of disaster, Mosey's respectfully restrained contribution patently reminds us that not all disasters are "natural". His compelling account of the terrorist murder of his daughter on Pan Am Flight 103 over the Scottish town of Lockerbie just prior to Christmas 1988, and of the effect this had upon himself, his wife, and his son, is an important ingredient to this book. Even disasters involving multiple fatalities – 270 in the case of the Lockerbie bombing – are deeply painful for each individual survivor, of which there were none in the Lockerbie bombing itself, and for each of the bereaved families involved, of which there were so many from the Lockerbie incident. Mosey takes the reader through the deeply moving and challenging journey he and his family have travelled. It is a journey they trod, armed with their strong Christian faith, through deep sorrow, and into some dark and disturbing areas of international politics. Striving to overcome evil with good through forgiveness, rather than being overcome by evil and bitterness, they also searched for justice for their beloved daughter.

Marie and Lucie's stories are reproduced, with their permission, from interviews held with them in Haiti, in 2013 and 2014, and are set in an ethnographic context of the common experience of womanhood in Haiti, both in pre- and post-earthquake eras. Their experience of surviving the catastrophe and life in an Internally Displaced Persons (IDP) camp is recounted in their own words to form a challenging and moving narrative of painful survival and resilience. Readers of this chapter are encouraged to carry with them the pertinent words of a Haitian diaspora, Brunine David, when he comments on typical ways Westerners think of resilience:

> When they dare to talk about our courage and strength or perseverance, they change the meaning and take all the good from it and leave us with resilience; a kind of people who accept any unacceptable situation, people who can live anywhere in any bad condition that no one else would actually accept.[1]

Honorat writes as a Haitian Christian pastor who is also a survivor of the catastrophic earthquake in the Caribbean country of Haiti in January 2010 (see Figure 0.1). He describes his upbringing

---

[1] Quoted in Gina Athena Ulysse, *Why Haiti Needs New Narratives: A Post-Quake Chronicle* (Middletown, CT: Weslyan University Press, 2015), p. 61.

in rural and then urban Haiti in a way that opens a window for the reader into the life of the average Haitian, into their culture, faith, and general daily living struggles and conflicts, to a way of life all too common in low-income countries. Then, in detail, he describes what it is like for such people to experience a powerful natural hazard like an earthquake when they are ill-prepared for it and also ill-equipped to respond and recover. Furthermore, he describes what it is like to live in a devastated country that has been "invaded" and "occupied" by so many international organizations, many of which have "parachuted" in with their short-term programmes and their big budgets, supposedly trying to help. He describes how that leaves a nation's people feeling, struggling to juggle gratitude with humiliation and despair. These are very painful lessons for both Haitians and for the international communities to learn.

When Hurricane Katrina, another natural hazard, swept into southern Louisiana from the Gulf of Mexico, back in late August 2005, it actually missed the city of New Orleans. Katrina was not to be the "Big One", the perfect storm, the worst-case scenario every New Orleanian dreads arriving: the one that hits the mouth of the Mississippi River head on and drives a storm surge up the river to overwhelm the levees that are built to contain it. As a moderated category 3 hurricane, it was strong, but not unusual or un-survivable. It did not hit the Mississippi head on, but veered to the north-east while still offshore. However, when the inevitable storm surge did come, it placed pressure on the drainage system's canal walls, supposedly built to mitigate flooding. Then the walls failed and the waters flooded 80 per cent of the city. If the result was not worst-case, it was not much less!

Taylor graphically describes for us what it means for a family to be flooded out of their home, out of their seminary, out of their church, and out of their city to seek refuge in neighbouring states. In particular, he relates the tale of how two churches, both devastated by "The Thing", as columnist and author Chris Rose wryly renamed the hurricane, came to be one church.[2] What was left of both congregations, came together to impact their community with their faith in action. He also describes how the Christian church, as a nationwide volunteer community, responded with skilful, life- and livelihood-saving professionalism, and with a godly heart to a disaster that exposed the deep cultural, racial, and political divisions in the city, state, and federal politics of the time.

From being exposed to the shocking realities of disaster bereavement and survival, and following some immersion in the historical and theological awareness of disasters that the Scriptures present us with, there is the contribution made by Rollinson regarding the emergence of the climate change crisis. By the time you are reading this book you will, more than likely, have read about, applauded or scoffed at, perhaps even been involved in the various protests and actions taken to raise the issue of climate change from the level of academic dispute, political indifference and inertia, and sheer public ignorance to the level of being a critical emergency in the minds of scientists and young people at least. This crisis may not seem as much for us personally as it does most certainly for the majority world of the poor. Though this subject was not covered in any focused way at the The Faraday Institute workshop, we felt it would be careless and foolish not to have a chapter, in a book of this nature, covering the climate change crisis.

Rollinson pleads with us to listen to the science and not to be deceived into believing it is just fake news – which is not always as easy as it may seem, given the climate change "doom dramatists" whose strategy can elevate fear above facts. The scientific facts Rollinson sets before readers are serious enough without their requiring such exaggerations that have no real foundation other than in scaremongering. The metaphor of our house being on fire as a consequence of global warming, although it may excite some

---

[2] Chris Rose, *1 Dead in the Attic: After Katrina* (New York: Simon and Schuster, 2007).

into thinking that a few degrees warmer for their summer holiday would be welcome, can only strike despair into those populations where increasing levels of drought and famine, together with the consequent food insecurity, are also leading to violence and war. Hence, Rollinson argues, climate change is not just a scientific and a truth issue, it is also a social justice matter, since it is the world's poor who stand to suffer most, even though they have contributed least to the causes.

Factual integrity, truth, and social justice are issues that should lie close to the hearts of Christians. Therefore, Rollinson concludes his chapter by venturing into the realms of theology. He believes we lack an appropriate theology, or that at the very least Christians can be slow and inadequate in applying an appropriate theology to the creation mandate and to the climate emergency. Certainly, he believes, any dilatory further attitudes will be dangerous and reneging on that creation mandate the Creator has given us: a mandate which means that one day we shall all have to account for our actions and attitudes.

Finally, as this book went to press, the COVID-19 pandemic struck the world. We have therefore added a final chapter on the pandemic and a Christian perspective on this global disaster. Doubtless many more books will be written on the medical, financial, social and personal impacts of COVID-19 in years to come. But in essence it highlights again the human factors involved in disasters and the way they expose the inequities and injustices in our societies.

Although this is by no means an exhaustive book on the subject of disasters, we believe it brings together an important collection of experiences and perspectives. We are thankful to God and to our participants at the workshop for enabling this to happen, both at the workshop and in this book. We believe the partnership of academics, responder–practitioners, and survivors working together is an essential strategy for a Christian response to disasters. We hope that by the end of this book, readers will agree.

# CHAPTER 1

# DISASTERS: NATURAL OR UNNATURAL?

## ROBERT WHITE

There is no such thing as a natural disaster.[1]

The world seems to be full of disasters, appearing on our TV screens and newspapers on a weekly basis. Some are clearly caused by humans: bridges fall down; buildings catch fire and incinerate many people; dams collapse and drown folk; terrorism and war inflict terrible suffering and atrocities. Others seem to be arbitrary, just "acts of God": earthquakes; volcanic eruptions; floods; outbreaks of highly infectious diseases. They are things that we feel should not happen in a well-ordered world. Yet they persist.

From a Christian perspective, the problem is especially pointed. Christians believe in an all-powerful, sovereign God, who is perfectly just and completely loving: so why does he permit disasters to happen? Indeed, all the monotheistic religions face the

---

[1] "It is generally accepted among environmental geographers that there is no such thing as a natural disaster. In every phase and aspect of a disaster – causes, vulnerability, preparedness, results and response, and reconstruction – the contours of disaster and the difference between who lives and who dies is to a greater or lesser extent a social calculus. Hurricane Katrina provides the most startling confirmation of that axiom", from Neil Smith, *There's No Such Thing as a Natural Disaster*, Understanding Katrina series, Items: Insights from the Social Sciences, Social Science Research Council, June 11, 2006, understandingkatrina. ssrc.org/Smith/ (last viewed 20 May 2019).

same knotty problem. Arguably, those with no faith commitment ought not to be so troubled, since there is then no reason why the world should be a just or a moral place; yet of course the pain, the suffering, and the tragedies are just as bad for everyone.

The problem has been debated and written about for millennia, so I do not claim to give any pat answers here. But nevertheless, there are some things we *can* say about the reasons for disasters. I will also review briefly what the writers of the Bible had to say about disasters: and they certainly knew all about them, because people in the Middle East where the biblical narrative unfolds have always experienced disasters, including famines, floods, earthquakes, and volcanic eruptions, on top of conflict and warfare.

In short, the message of this chapter is that what we call "natural" disasters – the floods, volcanic eruptions, and earthquakes – are the processes that make this world a fertile, habitable place where humans can thrive. These generally beneficial natural processes are frequently turned into disasters, primarily by the actions, or inactions, of humans. Thus, we might term them "unnatural disasters" rather than "natural disasters".

In the case of earthquakes, this is captured well by the aphorism "first the earthquake, *then* the disaster".[2] It has been applied many times, possibly starting with a 1970 earthquake in Peru which killed over 70,000 people. The disaster in Peru to which locals referred was the way in which subsequent heavily funded reconstruction and development programmes were directed from outside the affected communities by remote and aloof managers, with minimal regard for local leadership, organization, or community participation. In effect, they destroyed what had formerly been vibrant, self-driven, and motivated local networks and communities. We found exactly the same phenomenon in Haiti after the devastating 2010 earthquake that killed around 230,000 people: external aid agencies which flooded into the

---

[2] Paul L. Doughty (2005) "Learn from the past, be involved in the future", Human Organization, Winter Vol. 64, Iss. 4, pp. 303–15 (308).

country often ignored local expertise and knowledge, then in a relatively short time left the country, leaving the communities worse off than before (for more, see my co-authored title with Roger Abbott, *Narratives of Faith from the Haiti Earthquake*).

## The good Earth

On Christmas Eve 1968, the three crew members of the Apollo 8 spacecraft – Frank Borman, Bill Anders, and Jim Lovell – broadcast a last message before they traversed behind the Moon for the tricky manoeuvre of firing the retro-rockets manually to get them out of Moon orbit and on the way home. Anders began: "For all the people back on Earth the crew of Apollo 8 has a message we would like to send you". Then they read through the first ten verses of the book of Genesis, each in turn. Borman ended the broadcast: "From the crew of Apollo 8, we close with good night, good luck, a merry Christmas, and God bless all of you – all of you on the good Earth".

At the time, it was the biggest broadcast ever, estimated to have attracted an audience of about a billion people – one quarter of the global population. The iconic photograph taken on that same flight showing the earthrise of a richly coloured planet above a barren moonscape has become the most widely reproduced image in the world. It has been credited with kick-starting environmental concerns.

The sentiment the astronauts expressed of the inherent goodness of the Earth mirrors exactly the biblical view of creation. Six times in the first chapter of the Bible, after each creative day, God is reported as seeing all that he had made as "good". Then after he had made humans, "God saw all that he had made, and it was very good" (Genesis 1:31, NIV). There is not much mistaking the message of the goodness of creation.

There is, however, a catch. In the light of the disasters we experience around us, the world does not always feel as if it is good: it feels broken, somehow out of kilter. And the blame for that lies with humankind's rejection of God: what is often termed the "fall". The "goodness" of creation as described in Genesis is sometimes explained as a fitness for purpose. The created order fulfils, or begins to fulfil, God's intentions. Genesis and other biblical passages that describe the origins of creation provide the indispensable basis for any Christian discussion of how we relate to the rest of creation (for more, see my co-authored title with Jonathan A. Moo, *Hope in an Age of Despair*).

What about those natural processes that often create disasters: floods, volcanic eruptions, and earthquakes?

The most common disaster, which kills by far the most people, is flooding. Yet floods are a crucial means of distributing fertile soils eroded off mountains and deposited in river valleys, then used for agriculture. For millennia, it was the annual flood of the Nile that enabled Egypt to prosper. When the Nile flood failed, as for example in 1784, one-sixth of the population died.[3] A French traveller reported that "the Nile again did not rise to the favourable height, and the dearth immediately became excessive. Soon after the end of November, the famine carried off, at Cairo, nearly as many as the plague".[4]

Another natural hazard, volcanic eruptions, are crucial to the fertility of the Earth. They continually cycle to the surface from deep inside the Earth huge volumes of minerals essential for life. Volcanic islands such as Hawaii support lush growth of plants and animals, and are some of the most biodiverse areas on Earth. Volcanoes also provide the geological source of carbon dioxide in the atmosphere. Without that, the planet would probably have been frozen for most of its history. The average surface temperature in the absence of greenhouse gases such as

---

[3] Luke Oman et al. (2006) "High-latitude eruptions cast shadow over the African monsoon and the flow of the Nile", Geophysical Research Letters, Vol. 33, L18711, doi:10.1029/2006GL027665.

[4] M. C.-F. Volney, *Travels Through Syria and Egypt, in the Years 1783, 1784, and 1785. Containing the Present Natural and Political State of Those Countries,* translated from French (London: printed for G. G. J. and J. Robinson, 1787).

carbon dioxide in the atmosphere would be about $-6°C$ or lower.[5] This would have prevented the existence of most and maybe all of life, including humans. Yet volcanic eruptions may be explosively fatal to humans caught up in them.

Considering earthquakes as the last of this trilogy, they occur with a suddenness that is frequently catastrophic if they are near major cities. Yet without earthquakes there would be no plate tectonics and no mountain ranges. The continual building and erosion of mountains and the eruption of molten rock as part of the plate tectonic cycle provides a steady supply of nutrients which allows life to thrive. Another example of the role of mountains produced by the action of plate tectonics is that without the Himalayan mountain range the annual monsoons which provide water for 1 billion people in India would not occur. Mountain ranges, which grow through frequent earthquakes as the Earth's crust deforms, cause rainfall which in turn makes the land fruitful and habitable. These examples can be multiplied many times.

Although natural processes are beneficial in generating a suitable home for humanity, it is when humans interact poorly with them that a natural process can turn into a disaster.

## Disasters

A major factor, which makes disasters more devastating today than in the past, in terms of the numbers of people killed or affected, is the exponential increase in global population: there are almost five times as many people alive today as there were a century ago. Add to this the fact that more people now live in cities than in dispersed rural areas and that those cities are usually in river valleys or by the coast, and it is inevitable that large numbers of densely packed people are far more vulnerable to natural hazards than in the past.

---

[5] John Houghton, *Global Warming: The Complete Briefing* (Cambridge, UK: Cambridge University Press, Third Edition, 2004), p. 351.

Another critical factor is poverty: high-income nations and rich people can generally buy themselves out of trouble, either by building safe homes before a flood or earthquake, or by rebuilding afterwards. Poverty makes that much more difficult, though not impossible. In terms of losses, the lowest-income countries bear the greatest relative costs of disasters. Human fatalities and asset losses relative to gross domestic product are higher in the countries with the least capacity to prepare, finance, and respond to disasters.

Set against that vulnerability caused by population increase is an equally rapid increase in scientific understanding of how the natural world works. In principle, this means that natural hazards can be recognized and understood better, and as a result appropriate mitigation or adaptation strategies put in place. Key to this is education. Even the seemingly minor fact that 10-year-old Tilley Smith had heard about tsunamis from her geography teacher meant that she recognized the devastating Indian Ocean tsunami on Boxing Day 2004 as it approached the beach they were on. She was able to persuade her family and then others on the beach to move off it, saving maybe 100 lives.[6] The passing on of folk knowledge from previous generations who have faced similar hazards also has huge value.[7] Although the same tsunami killed over 230,000, people living on Simeulue island off the Sumatran coast, and the Moken people living in the Surin Islands off the coast of Thailand and Myanmar used knowledge passed on orally from their elders to survive it, despite being so close to the most affected areas. They knew that when the sea retreated suddenly, especially when it followed a period of earthquake shaking, then they should run immediately to high land. That knowledge saved their lives.

---

[6] *Lessons save lives: the story of Tilly Smith*, YouTube: https://www.youtube.com/watch?v=V0s2i7Cc7wA (last viewed 21 January 2020).
[7] United Nations Office for Disaster Risk Reduction (UNDRR) (2008), Indigenous knowledge for disaster risk reduction: good practices and lessons learned from experiences in the Asia–Pacific region, www.unisdr.org/files/3646_IndigenousKnowledgeDRR.pdf

## Earthquakes

Earthquakes cannot be predicted, but areas at risk are becoming understood better. Buildings and infrastructure can be built to be resilient against earthquakes, and to protect people. One of the triumphs of the 2011 Tohoku earthquake in Japan is that despite the magnitude 9.1 earthquake being 30 times larger than the maximum expected in this region, no one in Tokyo was killed by the earthquake because buildings did not fall down. And early warning systems that automatically detected the earthquake 12–15 seconds before the damaging surface seismic waves arrived applied emergency brakes that stopped 33 bullet trains travelling at average speeds of 300 km/hr. This saved many lives. Some 23,000 people unfortunately died from tsunami flooding: this wasn't due to a lack of awareness of the dangers of tsunami, but rather because it was even larger than expected or planned for. Ironically, some people lost their lives, despite there being adequate warnings, because they trusted too much in their tsunami protection walls, so did not try to escape to higher ground: indeed, some actually went down to the tsunami walls to watch the spectacle, with fatal consequences.

More shockingly, the likelihood of dying in an earthquake depends primarily on your poverty level or that of your country. A stark example is that the magnitude 7.0 earthquake in the low-income country of Haiti in January 2010 killed around 230,000, despite having 1,000 times less energy than the 2011 Tohoku earthquake. The deaths were caused primarily by poorly built buildings collapsing on top of people. It isn't that we don't know how to build earthquake-resistant buildings, as was demonstrated graphically by the fact that a 13-storey plate-glass-windowed skyscraper owned by the Digicel telecommunications company in Port-au-Prince survived without a single window being broken, while the newly built adjacent four-storey Turgeau hospital collapsed on top of many patients and medical workers (see Figure 1.1).

## Volcanoes

In general, volcanoes give warning signs before eruption which often allow people to evacuate safely. However, those warnings are sometimes purposely ignored, in which case there is no doubt that there is human culpability in the resultant deaths and injuries. A notorious example was the Mount St Helens eruption in 1980. Throughout March, seismic activity increased, with a small summit eruption on 27 March. By 30 April, local authorities had defined an exclusion zone extending 2–18 miles (3–30 km) from the volcano. But 83-year-old Harry Truman, who had lived at Spirit Lake for decades with his 16 cats, refused to leave. He was killed and buried under 150 ft (45 m) of ash when a cataclysmic eruption occurred on the morning of Sunday 18 May.

In Harry Truman's case, it was his own decision to stay, despite the efforts of the law enforcement officers to persuade him to leave. But a worse example, and the biggest volcanic disaster of the twentieth century, occurred on 8 May 1902. An estimated 26,000–36,000 people died when Mount Pelée in Martinique erupted violently at eight o'clock in the morning (according to Thomas and Morgan-Witts' *The Day Their World Ended*). All but one person died in Saint-Pierre, the largest city of Martinique, which was only 4 miles (6 km) from the foot of the volcano (see Figure 1.2). Yet there had been ample warning: the volcano had been spewing out ash and mud flows, with numerous earthquakes, for over two weeks. The city was chaotic, with water and food supplies failing, civil unrest, an outbreak of fever, and an influx of people from surrounding rural areas. Yet the governor actively prevented people leaving, even stationing soldiers to stop them walking the 11-mile (18 km) trail to the safety of the nearby commercial capital of Fort-de-France.

Why was the governor so keen to prevent people evacuating Saint-Pierre, against all common sense? The reason was that elections were due on 11 May, and the new socialist party which spoke primarily for the island's black and mixed-race majority looked set to wrest power from the conservative elite of white and

French expatriates. A large majority of the conservative voters lived in Saint-Pierre. The minister of colonies in France may have ordered the governor to keep Saint-Pierre's voters in town until the election was over (according to Solange Contour's *Saint-Pierre, Martinique, Vol. 2, La Catastrophe et ses suites,* 1989). In partial mitigation of the governor's actions, the ferocity and speed of the burning pyroclastic flows which overwhelmed Saint-Pierre was not well understood prior to the eruption. In fact, the volcano, Mount Pelée, thereafter gave its name to such volcanic flows: Peléan eruptions. In any case, it was an avoidable tragedy because the authorities first discouraged, then prevented, people leaving.

## Floods

Floods affect more people than all other natural disasters combined. On 12 November 1970, half a million people died in a single night from a flood in East Pakistan when the Bhola cyclone hit the coast. Numerous other examples occur every week, right down to the deaths of one or a few people when rivers burst their banks.

Floods disproportionately affect low-income countries and poor people, because high-income countries can protect themselves more effectively. Following tidal surges in 1953 which inundated large areas of eastern England and the Netherlands, killing 2,190 people, both the British and the Dutch built sea defences. The Thames Barrier and the Eastern Scheldt surge barrier are the largest moveable flood barriers on Earth, costing billions to build. But 30 million people living within one metre of sea level in the deltaic region of Bangladesh simply don't have the financial resources to build such barriers, even if it were technically feasible in a delta. There is a clear moral issue here: present rising sea levels and increasing intensity of storms are caused mainly by global climate change resulting from the burning of fossil fuels in high-income countries. But people in high-income countries are not usually the ones who suffer the worst consequences – the people most affected played little part in causing the problem in the first place, and have least resources to cope with it.

The way in which floods affect poor people most severely is also apparent when disaster strikes high-income, technologically advanced nations. In the floods caused by Hurricane Katrina in 2005, about 1,500 people died – they were disproportionately the infirm, the elderly, and the poor who could not leave the city as the storm approached.[8] Evacuation plans called for people to use their cars to drive away from the coastal areas at risk of flooding. That worked well for 80-90 per cent of the residents of New Orleans. But 112,000 people without access to personal vehicles were stranded.[9] For nearly a week after the hurricane, many of them were stuck in squalid conditions in overcrowded refuges and shelters before they were evacuated.

A report by the University of Louisiana into the causes of more than 50 breaches of the levees concluded that "failure of the NOFDS [New Orleans Flood Defense System] was a predictable, predicted, and preventable catastrophe". It continued: "this catastrophe did not result from an act of 'God'. It resulted from acts of 'People'".[10] Yet again, we see the same problem of human actions causing a preventable catastrophe.

## Climate change – a threat multiplier

Climate change is a major driver and amplifier of disaster losses. It amplifies risk and makes hitherto rare extreme events more common. Climate change contributes to, or exacerbates, many of the natural hazards we face: floods and droughts; high temperature extremes that cause sickness and even death for the very young and very old; rising sea levels as glaciers and ice caps melt, causing

[8] Tony Waltham (2005) "The flooding of New Orleans", Geology Today, Vol. 21, Iss. 6, pp. 225–31.

[9] B. Wolshon (2006) "Evacuation planning and engineering for Hurricane Katrina", The Bridge, Vol. 36, Iss. 1, pp. 27–34.

[10] Team Louisiana, *The Failure of the New Orleans Levee System during Hurricane Katrina* (Baton Rouge, LA: Louisiana Department of Transportation and Development, 2006), Appendix VI.

increased likelihood of flooding in coastal areas; declining and uncertain crop yields as weather patterns change and become more volatile; increased intensity of storms and hurricanes as the water vapour content of the atmosphere increases.

The occurrence of climate change caused by human activities has been measured and modelled by scientists for several decades, but it is now becoming apparent to everyone. Although many millions of years ago the Earth was sometimes hotter and sometimes cooler than now, the present climate change is happening at an unprecedented rate in human history. Carbon dioxide levels in the atmosphere, which are one of the main drivers of climate change, are higher than they have ever been since humans first walked on Earth. Dramatic weather events and volatile seasons are the new normal. Some climate change nay sayers will point to events such as the "Little Ice Age" during the mid-fifteenth to mid-nineteenth centuries, with temperatures so low that the River Thames in London froze over for weeks at a time, to suggest that such changes are simply part of the normal variability in the Earth's climate. But it is clear that those changes were regionally restricted, and at least partly driven by volcanic eruptions, whereas present climate changes are occurring across the entire globe.[11]

Again we see the moral issue: people in high-income countries have largely caused the climate changes by their burning of coal and hydrocarbons as a source of cheap energy, while those in low-income countries disproportionately suffer the consequences. There are certainly many ways to mitigate the risks of climate change, not only by reducing our burning of hydrocarbons and conserving energy or using it more efficiently, but also by developing drought-resistant crops, farming in ways that waste less water, eating less meat and more vegetable protein, developing better flood warning systems, and so on. Again, these

[11] Brönnimann et al. (2019) "Last phase of the Little Ice Age forced by volcanic eruptions", Nature Geoscience, Vol. 12, pp. 650–56.

are responses within the power of humans that will reduce or prevent disasters rather than sustaining the idea of "natural disasters" against which we are powerless.

## Some theological reflections

The Bible is suffused with descriptions of God not only as the Creator, but also as the sustainer of the entire cosmos, of both inanimate and living things: planets and stars and galaxies as well as quarks and photons; trees and animals as well as humans. The Bible leaves us in no doubt that God chose to make the cosmos, but himself existed before it, and that his creation was how he meant it to be – that it was fit for his purposes.

It is important, therefore, to remember that "nature" is not a force separate from God. We cannot say "nature caused that disaster" as if God had no part in it. John Wesley made this point after the catastrophic earthquake which flattened Lisbon in 1755 when he wrote in *Serious Thoughts Occasioned by the Late Earthquake in Lisbon*: "What is nature itself, but the art of God, or God's method of acting in the material world?" A similar idea was expressed over a millennium earlier by Augustine (AD 354–430) when he wrote that nature is what God has made (*De Genesi ad Litteram*). Natural processes occur under the overarching sovereignty of God, and so too must natural disasters. This should underpin our thinking.

But if God is good, indeed the very model of an all-loving, perfect Father, then why does he allow so-called natural disasters? It is worth commenting that we are quick to blame God for what we call natural disasters, while turning a blind eye to disasters which are undoubtedly caused by humans. For example, every year 1.35 million people die in car accidents: that is one every 23 seconds. Each one is a personal tragedy. In the USA as many folk die *every month* in car accidents as were killed in the Twin Towers terrorist atrocity of 9/11. Yet the latter is seared into the national consciousness and drove American intervention in Afghanistan with a long and costly war, whereas car accidents are accepted as simply a fact of life and are barely even reflected on other than by those directly affected. Or to take another example, pollution caused by human activities kills an estimated 4.5 million people annually (i.e. one person every seven seconds), yet it is largely avoidable.

Some Christian authors suggest that physical processes on Earth changed in a major way after humans rebelled against God in the Garden of Eden, writing that "earthquakes, volcanoes, floods and hurricanes were unknown before sin entered the world".[12] But geological observations show that there have been floods and tsunamis, earthquakes and volcanic eruptions since long before humans were present. Indeed, as already discussed, the very richness and fertility of this world which make it possible for humans to live and thrive is dependent on those same natural processes.

But the Bible writers do maintain that humankind's rebellion against God, portrayed in the first chapters of Genesis as the sin of Adam and Eve, has continued down throughout human history and in every generation and person since then. That breakdown in the proper relationship between the Creator God and ourselves also resulted in a breakdown of the relationship between ourselves and the rest of God's creation. This meant, for example, that growing food became a struggle and toil (Genesis 3:17–19). And the rest of creation was "subjected to frustration", as the Apostle Paul wrote in Romans 8:20. Human selfishness prevented the non-human creation playing its proper role of giving glory to God.

What went wrong, the Bible maintains, was that humans were not content to rule the world on behalf of God, as the first chapter of Genesis mandated. Instead, they wanted to be gods themselves, putting themselves in the place of God. They wanted to rule the world, whether their tiny patch, or with bigger ambitions, for their own selfish ends. The irony is that Adam and

---

[12] John Blanchard, *Where was God on September 11?* (Darlington, UK: Evangelical Press, 2002), p. 17.

Eve already had everything possible for fulfilled lives, living in harmony with both God and the rest of creation. Certainly, there was work to be done: they had to till the ground and take care of it (Genesis 2:15). Life was never intended to be one of hedonistic indulgence and idleness. Rather, God had entrusted care of the Earth to humans, who were made in his image. They exchanged all that for a lie. All the relationships between God, humankind, and the non-human creation were affected. Humans lost their immediate access to God, and the rightness and orderliness of life in the Garden of Eden. Their relationships with other people were spoiled, soon resulting in murder (Genesis 4:8) and fear of others, and spoiling the relationship between men and women (Genesis 3:16). That selfishness in the way humans often use creation for their own purposes is the root cause of why natural processes often turn into disasters.

The way we ought to rule over creation was modelled by Jesus when he was on Earth. Jesus rules as a pastor–king; as a shepherd who is in charge of and cares for his flock; a rule that is devoted to the good of others and the glorification of God the Father rather than serving his own ends. For humankind, this rule pre-echoes the new creation, where redeemed people will reign with Christ (2 Timothy 2:12; Revelation 5:9–10; 22:5). That is also why, although all of creation is presently "groaning as if in the pains of childbirth" (Romans 8:22, NIV), it is waiting "with eager longing for the revealing of the children of God", when it will be "set free from its bondage to decay" (Romans 8:19, 21).

Among many disasters which are recorded in the Bible, it is worth mentioning several that draw out some of the principles of how we might view them. The first is the seven-year famine in Egypt, recorded in the book of Genesis. Judah's son, Joseph, was sold by his brothers into slavery as a result of their jealousy, and imprisoned after being wrongfully accused of sexual misconduct. Eventually, his God-given foresight and administrative abilities enabled him to stockpile grain against the disaster of a seven-year famine. Many people from countries surrounding Egypt came to him for food, including those same brothers who had wronged him and had intended to kill him (Genesis 37:18). When Joseph eventually revealed himself to them, they thought that now they were going to suffer retribution for their cruelty 20 years earlier. But Joseph's response was that these events were actually all in God's providential oversight and intention. Three times over (in Genesis 45:5–8) Joseph tells his brothers that God had sent him to preserve life, eventually culminating in Genesis 50:19–20 (ESV): "As for you, you meant evil against me, but God meant it for good, to bring it about that many people should be kept alive, as they are today". The repeated emphasis certainly stresses the importance of this message. It neatly encapsulates the Bible's acceptance of and tension between the free will of humans and the sovereignty of God in all things, including disasters.

A second example is the experience of Job, recounted in the Old Testament book named after him. Job, a righteous worshipper of God and a very wealthy man, lost his livelihood, his wealth, his family, and even his health. Some of these disasters were due to natural causes, such as a house being blown down in a storm killing all his 10 children, whereas others were due to human evil such as the raids that killed his retainers and stole his livestock (Job 1:13–19). For 36 chapters, we then listen in as various "friends" tell Job generally unhelpful things such as that he must have committed some terrible sin, which is why he is suffering, that there must be some sin against God of which he hasn't repented (e.g. Job 4:7; 22:5), or more subtly that the righteous will prosper materially. But Job won't have any of it: he knows he is righteous, a view proclaimed three times over at the beginning of the book (Job 1:1, 8; 2:3), and a dozen times by Job. All Job wants is for God to explain himself, a very human response by almost everyone caught up in a disaster: "why me, O Lord?" we wail.

When God finally answers Job, he doesn't give some tidy explanation that explains why disasters happen. Instead, God gives a magnificent review of his creation and his sovereignty over the whole cosmos: from bringing into being the universe itself with its multitude of stars (Job 38:31-33); through the physical structure of the Earth (Job 38:4-18), its weather (Job 38:22-30, 34-38), and the animals and birds (Job 38:39-39:30); right down to care for what individual creatures eat (Job 38:39-41). God is sovereign over the most scary, untameable parts of his creation, and over evil itself. Job finally understands both that God's purposes cannot be thwarted and that God's knowledge and wisdom are far beyond anything to which Job could aspire. The lesson for us is that we should not and cannot expect to understand all of God's dealings this side of heaven. But we can and should hold on to God's faithfulness and goodness as Job did, however dire our circumstances may be.

As a final example, Jesus himself responded to questions about disasters when he was asked why 18 people had died when a tower in Siloam collapsed on them: we do not know the reason, but it may well have been in an earthquake since the Middle East is a seismically active area. Jesus used the disaster to teach again what we saw with Job, that there is no necessary connection between individual sinfulness and suffering. Jesus asks the rhetorical question "do you think that they were worse offenders than all the others who lived in Jerusalem?" and then answered it: "No, I tell you" (Luke 13:4-5). Then in his characteristic way Jesus went on to point beyond the immediate question that his hearers wanted answering to a much more important truth: "unless you repent, you too will all perish" (Luke 13:5, NIV). He reminds us of the reality of our need for God's mercy. It is striking that Jesus made exactly the same comment that "unless you repent, you too will all perish" when told about the death of Galileans at Pilate's orders (Luke 13:1-3, NIV). Those were deaths which were clearly caused by the evil of other people.

Throughout all these examples, we see God's sovereignty over both his creation and his people, even when people have acted in rebellion against him. But the last word is not with what goes wrong in the brokenness of this world we inhabit; rather it is with the good news that Jesus brings which gives real hope for the future, with its restoration of right relationships between God the Creator, his creation, and his people. We turn to this next.

## Hope for the future

The Christian gospel is woven through with hope not just for the present but also for the future. In the fullness of time, when Jesus returns, that new creation will be consummated and permanent. This provides a radically different perspective than the secular world can offer to the problem of disasters. In the face of a disaster, the secular world can only shake its head and say "we must do better next time". That is not much comfort to the bereaved and suffering.

It is often the poor who suffer most in disasters, so if those who are rich really did give generously to the poor it would have a big effect. Jesus is not being insensitive or making light of the very real sufferings caused by famines and shortage of food when he tells us not to worry about what we will eat. But he does throw us back on dependence on God rather than thinking we can rule the world, or even rule our own little domains ourselves however we please; practical experience over millennia shows that our sinful natures mean that we cannot do that in a just and equitable way.

The Christian perspective sees the reality of the brokenness of this world, but also the truth of God's sovereignty over it and of his ultimate plans for a new creation. That does not mean that we need not strive to improve things now. Rather it points in the opposite direction, that we should work for better scientific understanding of disasters, that we should enable communities to build resilience against them, that we should strive to remove the unjust disparities in wealth and resources that mean it is so often the poor who are most vulnerable and who suffer most. Even though we may not be able to prevent every last casualty of the next disaster, there is an enormous amount we can do even from our present understanding of natural processes to reduce hugely the impact of disasters. This is surely what Jesus would want us to do, using our understanding of his creation for the good of others and working to enable his creation to reflect his glory as he intended it to.

# CHAPTER 2

# DISASTERS, INJUSTICE, AND THE GOODNESS OF CREATION

## JONATHAN MOO

The need to think carefully about how to interpret and respond to disasters has sadly never been greater. One of the effects of climate change and the increasingly degraded ecosystems of our age is an increased likelihood of and susceptibility to disasters, the causes of which are rarely simply "natural" but instead are nearly always linked to a mix of human and "natural" factors. In this chapter, I explore how disasters are portrayed in Scripture and suggest that the category of "apocalypse" best describes the way that disasters serve to reveal the power of God and the limits of humanity, while exposing injustice and judging evil. Most importantly, I consider the response to the threat of disaster to which God's people are called, as seen through a few biblical examples and especially God's own response in the person of Jesus Christ.

Disasters regularly provoke absurd and unhelpful responses in their immediate aftermath, usually from those not caught up in the disaster themselves. The responses, whether from secular or religious people, seem to indicate that this or that most recent disaster is the first time they have confronted the reality of a world full of death and suffering. Any academic investigation of disasters is thus haunted by a long history of counterproductive and downright harmful attempts to explain suffering and loss, a history that goes back at least to the friends of the biblical Job and that continues in the caricature of the "best-of-all-possible-worlds" arguments attacked by Voltaire after the Lisbon earthquake of 1755. Similar "explanations" continue to be heard today in the sort of facile invocations of God's judgment that certain Christian preachers are prepared to trot out after every hurricane and earthquake. It's a trope that secular environmentalists also borrow, simply replacing the judgment of God with the judgment of nature or Gaia.

It is therefore necessary to begin an investigation like this one with a caveat. "Disasters" are not merely another academic subject to be studied and analyzed. Theologically they confront us with questions about evil for which no merely academic answer is satisfactory; and personally they confront us with experiences of suffering and loss before which words always fall short. Nonetheless, it is important for Christians to take advantage of times when we are not caught up in the suffering that a disaster involves to reflect carefully on the nature of God's world and what sort of people we are called to be in the light of the God who is revealed to us in Jesus Christ. There are implications not only for how we might hope to respond when disaster inevitably does strike, but also for what is required of us now to mitigate the possibility of disaster before it happens.

This chapter is necessarily a 30,000-ft view of the subject, trying to summarize something of the entire biblical witness and to consider in general terms its possible implications. Such an approach cannot stand alone, however. Readers are urged to read this alongside the chapters in this volume written by those who have more sustained and direct experience of working on the frontlines of disaster.

## Defining disaster

There are many references in Scripture to droughts, earthquakes, and volcanoes; to accidents; and to more obviously human-caused disasters such as war, terrorism, and state-sponsored violence. Yet these exist on a continuum with and are not sharply distinguished from everyday smaller-scale loss and devastation.

There is not even a specific vocabulary for "disaster": destructive and fatal events, large or small, are all simply described as "bad" or "evil" things (Hebrew: *ra'a*'; Greek: *kakos*). Thus, although the responses required will obviously vary with the scale – and, in our contemporary context, aid agencies necessarily work with more precise definitions – the operative principles and the theological questions raised by disasters large and small are much the same. Hence, stories like that of Job's individual experience of loss and devastation are relevant for our examination of Scripture's portrayal of disaster, as are biblical references to such things as predators, parasites, and other small-scale "natural" causes of loss.

Incidentally, the previous chapter by Robert White in this book challenges on empirical grounds the notion that there is a separate category of "natural" disaster, given that human factors nearly always play a significant role in the loss of life that such events involve. This is consistent with how the Christian Scriptures envision the entanglement of the natural and the human, where there is none of modernity's artificial attempt to divide nature and culture. It is also, as we will see, consistent with the moral imperative to expose and address the human sources of injustice and inequality that nearly always exacerbate or cause outright those things we call "disasters" or "acts of God". Nonetheless, it is necessary to acknowledge that, however much we might be able to prevent the loss of life and property that such things as earthquakes and volcanoes cause (if we actually acted on what we knew and made perfectly just and right decisions), the very existence of such death-dealing parts of creation and the potential loss of even one life raise important questions for a Christian doctrine of creation.

## On (not) explaining disaster

Behind all Christian discussions of disaster looms the question of how to reconcile the existence of a good and powerful God with the reality of evil and suffering. Though I will not attempt an answer here, I do consider it necessary to rule out one popular but unhelpful and unsatisfactory answer. This is the temptation to link volcanoes, earthquakes, storms, hurricanes, and creatures that harm and kill human beings to a cosmic fall, to the results of humanity's rejection of God. Especially since the Reformation, this has been perhaps the dominant explanation offered for what is sometimes called natural evil and hence for disasters of all kinds. Romans 8:18–25 is sometimes thought to offer evidence for this link, but it is better understood as testifying to the frustration of creation's purpose due to its subjection to human beings who in their sinfulness lead to its ruin and groaning.[1]

Most famously, John Calvin, in his commentary on Genesis, provides a rather extensive list of things that he considers only to have come onto the scene with the fall of humanity described in Genesis 3. Calvin's list ranges from potential causes of disaster to creatures which he apparently simply found to be unpleasant:

> It appears that all the evils of the present life, which experience proves to be innumerable, have proceeded from the same fountain. The inclemency of the air, frost, thunders, unseasonable rains, drought, hail, and whatever is disorderly in the world, are the fruits of sin. Nor is there any other primary cause of diseases.
>
> … many things which are now seen in the world are rather corruptions of it than any part of its proper furniture. For ever since man declined from his high original, it became necessary that the world should gradually degenerate from its nature. We must come to this conclusion respecting the existence of fleas, caterpillars, and other noxious insects. In all these, I say, there is some deformity of the world, which

---

[1] For details, see Jonathan Moo (2018) "From ruin to renewal: the groaning of creation under human dominion", Sapienta, Vol. 7: http://henrycenter.tiu.edu/2018/09/from-ruin-to-renewal; and Jonathan Moo (2008) "Romans 8.19–22 and Isaiah's cosmic covenant", *New Testament Studies*, Vol. 54, pp. 74–89.

ought by no means to be regarded as in the order of nature, since it proceeds rather from the sin of man than from the hand of God.[2]

I should note that Calvin immediately qualifies that these things were indeed created by God. But they were created not as good things but as "Avengers", as things to punish us and remind us of our sin.

The use of a cosmic fall as an explanation for disaster and so-called natural evil is disarmingly simple. But it flies in the face of absolutely everything we know about life on Earth. As others before me have observed, you can't help but wonder if Calvin had as negative a view of butterflies as he did of caterpillars. It is difficult to overstate the ways in which everything upon which we depend in creation, from the fruitfulness of the Earth to its moderate climate to all those things which we love and celebrate in the natural world, are all inextricably linked to such things as the movement of tectonic plates, volcanoes, floods, and, in the biotic realm, on the cycle of life and death. Much more generally, any world with gravity and trees and water must be a world with at least *potential* risk. Whatever sort of a pre-fall world is imagined by those who link all that is potentially harmful or threatening to some sort of a historical cosmic fall is certainly not any version of the current world that we would recognize.

But it's not necessary to belabour the point, because for Christians there is a more fundamental problem with any attempt to link all that is dangerous and wild and potentially death-dealing in our world to a cosmic fall. The problem is that Scripture itself contradicts it. There is no sense in Scripture of the sort of radical rupture in the non-human creation itself between a pre-fall state and what exists now. And it is not just recent or post-Darwinian interpreters who have recognized that fact.

---

[2] John Calvin, *Commentary on Genesis* (trans. John King; Grand Rapids, MI: Christian Classics Ethereal Library), pp. 62–63, 117. Available at http://www.ccel.org

To take one of my favourite examples, here is what the great fourth-century Cappadocian, Basil of Caesarea says in his sermon series on Genesis: "Each of the things that have been made fulfils its own particular purpose in creation... Not a single one of these things is without worth, not a single thing has been created without a reason". For Basil, included among these "treasures of creation" are even those plants and animals that are harmful to human life: "Shall we give up acknowledging our gratitude for those things that are beneficial and reproach the Creator for those that are destructive of our life?" Basil's wonder at creation included all creatures, even the "scorpion's delicate stinger, which the Craftsman hollowed out like a pipe to throw venom into those it wounds. And let nobody reproach him on account of what he made, because he brought forth venomous animals, destructive and hostile to our life". Even though these creatures sometimes cause harm to people, they nonetheless testify to God's creative goodness in and of themselves.[3]

Basil gets this idea from Scripture itself. In the context, he is simply expounding on what he finds in the early chapters of Genesis, and he sees no reason to exclude any parts of the wondrous, even dangerous, world of living, creeping, and crawling creatures from the goodness of creation pronounced seven times in the first chapter of the Bible. Basil says that there could never be enough time to recount all the wonders of creation, quoting Psalm 104:24 (NIV): "How many are your works, LORD! In wisdom you made them all; the earth is full of your creatures".

This is an instructive text, because of all the psalms, it is Psalm 104 that confirms that this world in which we now live – even with all its dangers – remains the good world of God's creation and the arena of God's glory. It is a comprehensive vision,

---

[3] This is adapted from my discussion in D. J. Moo and J. A. Moo, *Creation Care: A Biblical Theology of the Natural World* (Grand Rapids, MI: Zondervan, 2018), pp. 99–100. The translations of Basil (from the *Hexaemeron*) are my own.

including those wildest parts of the world and those creatures and phenomena that in other contexts threaten civilization and human life. Everything from lions (Psalm 104:20–21) to Leviathan (verse 26), from earthquakes to volcanoes (verses 31–32), is celebrated as part of God's good creation; in wisdom, he made it *all* (verse 24). These same themes emerge in God's speeches to Job, wherein Job is forced to confront the reality of a world that eludes complete human understanding and control, a world that exists first and last for God and not for ourselves.

What, then, of the "fall" and disasters and suffering? I have written more extensively on this topic elsewhere,[4] but for the purposes of this chapter, it suffices to observe the following:

- Scripture confirms and confronts the reality of suffering and death, names it as an evil, and claims that death is the last enemy.
- Nonetheless, Scripture never portrays the wildness of creation, including those natural processes that are often triggers of disaster and suffering, as evil in and of themselves. In fact, these are celebrated as parts of God's good world.
- Scripture portrays a future new creation where suffering, sickness, and death will be no more – where death will be destroyed. But this new creation is not simply a return to first conditions, a going back to Genesis 1–2. It is rather a taking of this creation to the ends for which God always intended it, a realization of its *telos* (end/purpose) that could come only through Christ.

For Irenaeus, writing in the late second century, this world is therefore to be seen as good but not perfect. It is a training camp, as it were, for the new creation to come. Athanasius too recognized that natural death itself, for example, is a part of the

---

[4] See Moo and Moo, *Creation Care*, pp. 99–113; and Jonathan Moo (2018) "From ruin to renewal", *Sapientia*: https://henrycenter.tiu.edu/2018/09/from-ruin-to-renewal/

givenness of the created order. Therefore, life without death can be only an *additional* gift of grace, something new in the order of things. Death and corruption is the natural law, the way of things; it was only in the Garden of Eden (and in the hoped-for future) that humanity might be protected within a world such as this and given the gift of life without death. Thomas Aquinas similarly developed this theme as his explanation for what some call "natural evil": if humanity lived in obedience to God, then God would by his grace supply power, "a special and supernatural act of his kindness", to live in this creation in a way that disaster and harm could not hurt us (*Summa Contra Gentiles*, Book IV, ch. 52).

The point I am attempting to make all too briefly here has recently been articulated by Jonathan Wilson as follows:

> [S]in and death are not the result of the fall away from an original perfection. Rather, sin and death are the consequence of and evidence of the turn away from, resistance to, and rebellion against the telos of creation. In other words, the fall is a rejection of God's purposes for life. It is best understood not as a corruption of the original but as the disruption and deflection of the completion of creation in eternal life, which is the new creation. One way of expressing this is to say that in its beginning creation was teleologically perfect, not originally perfect. In other words, God made the cosmos perfectly suited for the fulfilment of its purpose in Jesus Christ. This is not a proclamation of the imperfection of creation but a recasting of what "the perfection of creation" means.[5]

In summary, I am suggesting that we not allow the fact that Christianity has always named evil as evil, and death as contrary to

---

[5] Jonathan R. Wilson, *God's Good World: Reclaiming the Doctrine of Creation* (Ada, MI: Baker Academic, 2013), p. 119.

God's final purpose for us, to distort our vision of the goodness of this given creation now and during our ordinary, limited human life. (For more on this, see Ephraim Radner's *A Time to Keep: Theology, Mortality, and the Shape of a Human Life*.) We are left with unanswered questions about why God would create such a world in the first place, a world where the very processes that bring life are inevitably conjoined with processes of death and decay, a world that is good but not perfect. Theologians have attempted a variety of answers to such questions. One partial but necessary answer is that disaster and suffering and death will not have the last word; Scripture claims that there will be a new creation where there will be no more death or pain (e.g. Revelation 21:4). But the key is that this end is not simply a return to the beginning; biblical faith is not a myth of eternal return. The Christian's orientation toward this world is directed not back to some mythical primeval state to which we are always attempting to return. Rather, we begin here and now, where we are, acknowledging our limits and constraints, and the mystery and power of a creation that at once awes and confounds us. At the same time, we press for justice and righteousness, the preservation of life, the alleviation of suffering, and the embodying of love, knowing that this is the work of the new creation secured for us in Christ.

## Disaster as apocalypse

Beyond the basic sorts of definitions of disaster that agencies like the Red Cross use to determine when outside assistance is necessary, there is recognition in the academic literature on disasters that the events that we consider to be the *causes* of disaster are more accurately described as the "triggers" or "revealers" of pre-existing situations of injustice and inequality. For example, the website for the Aarhus University Laboratory for Past Disaster Science notes the following:

> Large-scale and potentially destructive environmental events
> such as volcanic eruptions, earthquakes, and tsunamis have

happened throughout human history and prehistory. Yet, disasters are generated only in the interplay between such events and the human societies they impact.[6]

In a similar vein, anthropologist and historian Virginia Garcia-Acosta observes:

Since disasters serve as social laboratories, revealers, and sometimes triggers of critical pre-existing situations, emphasis should be placed on understanding the surrounding and prior sociocultural context and vulnerability to the effects of a certain hazard.[7]

This notion that disasters reveal pre-existing situations is consonant with the biblical understanding of disaster. In what follows, I will briefly explore this idea of disaster as "apocalypse", intending by "apocalypse" to invoke the sense the word has in Koine Greek: a "revealing" or "unveiling". In Scripture, disasters reveal the power of God and the limits of human power and understanding; but they also reveal either the faithfulness and resilience of human individuals and communities or their evil, injustice, and inequality.

It is in Job above all that we see how disaster can reveal God's power and the ineffably mysterious nature of God's ways. Job has suffered his own disaster, and though he does not get an answer to the question of why he is suffering, the answer he does get is in the person of a God who *is* finally just, but whose purposes cannot always be discerned nor understood by Job or anyone else. And it is above all in the created world and all its wildness that Job can learn this.

---

[6] See https://projects.au.dk/lapadis/

[7] Virginia Garcia-Acosta, "Historical Disaster Research" in *Catastrophe & Culture: The Anthropology of Disaster* (eds. Susanna M. Hoffman and Anthony Oliver-Smith; Santa Fe, NM: School of American Research Press, 2002), p. 65. Used with permission.

The divine speeches (Job 38–41) present Job with a series of questions that highlight what Job does not and cannot know about creation and the profound limitations of his power. By confronting Job with the irreducible mystery of the cosmos and its creatures, God reminds him (and us) of the limitations of Job's power and wisdom, limitations that could never be overcome simply by accumulating more information. Even if Job should, for example, become a wildlife biologist and learn "when the mountain goats give birth" and see when "the doe bears her fawn" (39:1, NIV), the lives of other creatures always remain finally inaccessible to us. Part of the reason for such mystery is that creation, in all its wonder and wildness, does not exist to serve Job and humankind. Hence the emphasis on creatures who laugh at settled human life, whose homes – like the eagles and the mountain goats – are in wild and inaccessible places, and who – like the lions and Behemoth and Leviathan – are in fact threats to life and property, and yet for whom God provides, just as he does for the uninhabited desert. Even the wildest and most threatening and uncontrollable parts of creation were created by God, right alongside Job (40:15). Inscrutable or terrifying as they may be, they exist to fulfil God's purposes and bring God glory.

One of the purposes of this apocalyptic unveiling of God's power and human limits is the reminder that the only one who can save is the God for whom even Behemoth and Leviathan are but playthings. The appropriate response to this is repentance (42:6). In Job's case, it is not a matter of repenting of sin but of the presumption to understand and control what can never be fully known or controlled. Job had sought to speak "of things I did not understand, things too wonderful for me to know" (42:3, NIV).

Perhaps in our own age, in the so-called Anthropocene (the geological era in which humans have a dominant influences on the climate and environment – see Mark Lynas' *The God Species*) in which some claim to be able to harness humankind's newfound knowledge and power to shape the world according to their whims, one of the necessary roles of the risk of disaster is to recall us to a more humble and realistic understanding of the limits of our knowledge and power. Indeed, the restraint that such a recognition, guided by wisdom, might recall us to may be one of the things most necessary to save us from many of the disasters that currently threaten civilization and the flourishing of life.

In addition to revealing God's power and human limits, disaster serves in Scripture to reveal the true condition of human beings. On the one hand, a disaster can reveal the faithfulness and resiliency of an individual or community. The disasters that strike Job, for example, reveal him to be a faithful truth-teller (e.g. Job 42:7). Even through all his suffering and wrestling with God, his faith is found to be genuine. In the New Testament, 1 Peter describes suffering as a testing by fire, praying that "the genuineness of your faith—being more precious than gold that, though perishable, is tested by fire—may be found to result in praise and glory and honor when Jesus Christ is revealed" (1 Peter 1:6–7). This theme is echoed in 2 Peter, describing the fiery day of the Lord as a time when "the earth and everything that is done on it will be disclosed" (2 Peter 3:10), and encouraging readers to faithfulness: "Therefore, beloved, while you are waiting for these things, strive to be found by him at peace, without spot or blemish" (3:14). The aim is to be prepared for disaster, for suffering, and for the day of the Lord by being faithful, embodying the virtues of God's kingdom (see also 2 Peter 3:11–12). In Revelation, Jesus commends those in the churches John addresses who have been found faithful in the face of severe economic hardship, persecution, and even threatened martyrdom (e.g. Revelation 2:13).

On the other hand, and inevitably more often, disasters serve in Scripture to reveal (and judge) evil, injustice, and inequality. The flood is the quintessential example. Note how the Hebrew narrator of Genesis 6:12–13 suggests that even God's judgment here can be described as a revealing of what is already the case

And God saw that the earth was corrupt [corrupted/ ruined]; for all flesh had corrupted [/ruined] its ways upon the earth. And God said to Noah, "I have determined to make an end of all flesh, for the earth is filled with violence because of them; now I am going to destroy [corrupt/ruin] them along with the earth".

In the story of the Exodus, readers are again reminded that God's judgment is an enactment of justice, and the natural world is enlisted to expose and fight back against the evil ends to which it has been put. For example, the Pharaoh has thrown Hebrew baby boys into the Nile, ostensibly the source of life in Egypt (Exodus 1:22). In the series of disasters that God then brings upon the Egyptians, the Nile turns to blood (Exodus 7:17–18).

Most often, it is God's own people who experience disaster as a result of God's judgment. To take one of countless examples, here is Jeremiah's interpretation of the ruin of Judah and Jerusalem from Jeremiah 9:11–14:

> I will make Jerusalem a heap of ruins, a lair of jackals; and I will make the towns of Judah a desolation, without inhabitant. Who is wise enough to understand this? To whom has the mouth of the LORD spoken, so that they may declare it? Why is the land ruined and laid waste like a wilderness, so that no one passes through? And the LORD says: Because they have forsaken my law that I set before them, and have not obeyed my voice, or walked in accordance with it, but have stubbornly followed their own hearts and have gone after the Baals, as their ancestors taught them.

There is an assumed connection here and elsewhere in Scripture between so-called natural disasters and the faithfulness of God's people. The principle is one that we do well to acknowledge, for example, by seeking the social-political-individual factors inevitably involved in disasters and accepting our own culpability and involvement even in so-called natural disasters. But it's also vital to acknowledge that such judgments are described in the Hebrew Bible in connection to the nation of Israel and the nations with which it interacted; and it is the biblical prophets who interpret for us the significance of the disasters described. None of us live in ancient Israel nor have the insight of Hebrew prophets. We are therefore never in a position to attribute a disaster directly to the judgment of God. Moreover, as Jesus reminds his disciples (Luke 13:1–4), some disasters are truly random, the result of living in this sort of world, a good but not perfect world.

Unsurprisingly, it is in the Apocalypse of John, the book of Revelation, where my theme of disaster as apocalypse becomes especially clear. John challenges his readers to perceive the lies behind the violence, oppression, inequality, and economic exploitation of Rome. And one of the ways he does that is by describing in his visions a world where things fall apart; where the peace that Rome claimed to have brought is shown to be a lie; where the skewed economic priorities of Rome are exposed; and where the magic spell cast by Rome's power and wealth is broken, and the city of violence is thrown down (see especially chapters 6 and 18). Interestingly, at the centre of John's vision of the defeat of the powers of evil, it is the beast itself that destroys Babylon (17:16–17). John is perceiving an inherent instability in evil that ultimately brings disaster upon itself.

## Responding to disaster

Whatever the ultimate or proximate causes of disaster, and whatever is thereby revealed, the focus in Scripture is on the response demanded of God's people. After Israel's defeat by Midian, Gideon asks the sort of question we all might ask: "But sir, if the LORD is with us, why then has all this happened to us?" (Judges 6:13) Tellingly, Gideon receives not an answer but a commission: "Then the LORD turned to him and said, 'Go in this might of yours and deliver Israel from the hand of Midian; I hereby commission you'" (verse 14). Similarly, when Jesus' disciples ask him to explain why a man was born blind, assuming that someone must have sinned for such evil to have befallen him, Jesus' answer shifts their focus: "Neither this man nor his parents sinned; he was born blind so that God's works might be revealed in him. We must work the works of him who sent me while it is day" (John 9:3–4). In fact, the NRSV translation supplies words that are missing in the Greek text, and the verse might alternatively be translated: "Neither this man nor his parents sinned; but, so that God's works might be revealed in him, we must work the works of him who sent me while it is day". The point is that simplistic explanations for disaster are ruled out, and the challenge to Jesus' disciples is to do the work to which they are called. When it comes to disaster and the threat of disaster, Scripture suggests that the response to which God's people are called will include: lament, humility, the preservation of life, repentance, and hope.

## Lament

God's response to disaster, even disaster that is the result of God's own judgment, is lament. Thus, in the same passage quoted before about God's judgment of Judah and Jerusalem, God says, "I will weep and wail for the mountains and take up a lament concerning the wilderness grasslands. They are desolate and untravelled, and the lowing of cattle is not heard. The birds have all fled and the animals are gone" (Jeremiah 9:10, NIV; see also Isaiah 16:6–11). The prominence of lament throughout Scripture and the example of Jesus himself (e.g. Luke 19:41; John 11:35) indicates the prominent place it ought to have in the Christian church's response to disaster.

## Humility

Alongside lament is the need for humility, as we have seen in the example of Job. Humility is necessary if we are to fulfil our central task in responding rightly to disaster by preserving life. In cultivating an appropriate awe before God and his creation, we are reminded that we are not the saviours of the world and that there are always limits to our understanding and power.

The illusion of perfect control otherwise too often leads us to do greater damage – as is likely for many of the proposals to use geoengineering to save us from climate change, for example. There is also the risk of misidentifying the good, as I am reminded now each summer as historically catastrophic wildfires erupt in my part of the world (western North America) after a century of misguided wildfire suppression. Regular small fires are necessary to the health of forests here, yet we mistook them for evils to be stopped, and now we suffer the consequences of our mistake, compounded by the effects of an ever-warming climate. In my research for this chapter, I encountered a well-known biblical scholar who misreads Jesus' point in Matthew 5:45, where Jesus says that God "sends rain on the righteous and on the unrighteous" (NIV). Jesus' point is that God liberally pours out blessings on all. Yet this scholar (who shall go unnamed), apparently adopts the standpoint of an inconvenienced picnicker rather than a Middle Eastern farmer and cites it as an example of how bad things happen to everyone.

## The preservation of life

So humility is important. Yet we can't stop here and merely gaze in wonder at a world beyond our knowledge and control. Humility must be joined to a significant sense of responsibility lest it become merely an excuse to remain in wilful ignorance of the human role in disaster and in such things as contemporary climate change. As has already been observed, disasters are rarely simply "natural" events for which we bear no culpability; when the wildness of a world with earthquakes and storms and volcanoes leads to human suffering and death, most often the suffering and death is preventable. Whatever the cause of disaster, the example of Jesus shows Christians what our response must always be: healing, restoration, and justice.

In the disaster that God brings upon the Earth in the flood, the only role given to his servant Noah is to preserve life, "to keep alive" all the creatures, a refrain repeated in the story three times (Genesis 6:19–20; 7:3). Later in Genesis, Joseph, facing a disastrous famine, is given the same commission: "to preserve life" and "to keep alive" (Genesis 45:5–7). Protection and preservation of life in the face of disaster is how God's people embody the love, justice, and righteousness in which God delights (Jeremiah 9:23–24). If God is "a refuge to the poor, a refuge to the needy in their distress" (Isaiah 25:4), so too are God's people called to be, even in the welcome of the foreigner and refugee whose homeland has become uninhabitable: "Give counsel, grant justice; make your shade like night at the height of noon; hide the outcasts, do not betray the fugitive; let the outcasts of Moab settle among you; be a refuge to them from the destroyer" (Isaiah 16:3–4). In Matthew 25:35–36 Jesus shows us what such compassion and generous welcome looks like, and calls his followers to the same practice:

> I was hungry and you gave me food, I was thirsty and you gave me something to drink, I was a stranger and you welcomed me, I was naked and you gave me clothing, I was sick and you took care of me, I was in prison and you visited me.

There are examples in the New Testament of how the early church sought to live this out. Thus, a famine during the reign of Claudius leads the disciples to determine that "according to their ability, each would send relief to the believers living in Judea; this they did, sending it to the elders by Barnabas and Saul" (Acts 11:29–30). The goal, Paul would say, is equality, telling the Corinthians, "At the present time your plenty will supply what they need, so that in turn their plenty will supply what you need. The goal is equality" (2 Corinthians 8:14, NIV).

The promoting of life and the flourishing of all members of a community that is intrinsic to righteousness, and the establishment of order and protection of the weak that is a requirement of justice, begins long before disaster strikes. The expression of God's love and compassion in preserving and promoting the flourishing of life that is the duty of God's people therefore also requires preventing and preparing for disaster. Scripture hints at the responsibility that God's people have to prevent misfortune before it even happens. Thus, for example, "When you build a new house, you shall make a parapet for your roof; otherwise you might have bloodguilt on your house, if anyone should fall from it" (Deuteronomy 22:8). A simple precaution, perhaps, but there are wider implications here for how God's people invest in those things that protect others from harm. In other cases, such as that of Joseph, disaster is simply expected: a famine will come. So, to prepare for the preservation of life, steps are taken to store up food and get ready for what is known to be coming.

The example of Joseph is also a cautionary tale, however. The buying up of grain that he orchestrated to prepare for famine led to the centralization of power and the accumulation of wealth in the hands of a few. In the end, "the land became Pharaoh's. As for the people, he [Joseph] made slaves of them from one end of Egypt to the other" (Genesis 47:20–21). In the narrative of the Pentateuch (Genesis to Deuteronomy), this sets up the situation that we encounter at the beginning of Exodus, where the Hebrews are enslaved under a new pharaoh who knows nothing of Joseph (Exodus 1:8–11). There is a reminder here that the way in which we give help obviously matters. It is possible in providing short-term relief to serve unjust systems that merely set up future disasters – as in our day the proliferation of "disaster capitalism" makes all too clear (for more, see Naomi Klein's *The Shock Doctrine*). Disasters are not an excuse to abandon the principles of love, righteousness, justice, and equality, but a call to embody them all the more.

## Repentance and hope

Finally, in Scripture the prospect of disasters serves above all as a reminder of our ongoing need for repentance, a reason always to examine our lives and to turn to the only source of our hope and salvation. In revealing to us again our limits and our fragility, disasters force us to ask in whom or in what we place our trust (see Luke 8:24–25; Revelation 6:17). God's own response to disaster is the cross of Jesus Christ. God enters into the suffering of the world, defeats the powers of death, and opens the way of life to a new creation where disaster will be no more. In this is our hope, and our commission.

# CHAPTER 3

# "WHAT GOOD IS GOD?" DISASTERS, FAITH, AND RESILIENCE

## ROGER ABBOTT

I n the preceding two chapters, drawing on history and theology respectively, both authors have affirmed the goodness of the creation, but they have also affirmed that the creation as we now see it and experience it does not always appear to match up to such an affirmation. Life now is "not the way it's supposed to be", as Cornelius Plantinga states it.[1] This "catch", as Robert White terms the mismatch, in fact is a view of life that the Scriptures paint for us very graphically. Life as we know it on Earth can be dangerous and painful, and never more so than when the creation itself seems to become, in the words of social anthropologist Anthony Oliver-Smith, the "angry earth" (see his book of the same name), or, as Pope Paul II called it, "a rebellion on the part of nature".[2] This chapter attempts to explore how both theology and the narrative experience of survivors addresses the above "catch".

In Christian circles it is often said, almost as a kind of mantra at times, "God is good!... All of the time!" We Christians

---

[1] Cornelius Plantinga Jr. (ed.), *Not the Way it's Supposed to be: A Breviary of Sin* (Grand Rapids, Michigan: Eerdmans, 1997).

[2] John Paul II, Encyclical Letter *Centesimus Annu* 37: AAS 83 (1991), p. 840, cited in Francis Encyclical Letter, *Laudato Si* of the Holy Father Francis. 1st ed. (2015), p. 88.

can be good nowadays at constructing religious mantras, as if we needed to convince ourselves that we do still believe certain things to be true, and that repeating things over and over is a safe form of truth formation! That said, in Christian theology, the goodness of God is a fundamental ontological attribute of God; it is what God is. When it comes to disasters however, this attribution of goodness can be severely challenging, and never more so than when children and the "defenceless" suffer and/ or die. For some people, such disasters can even fit the category of "horrendous evils". These evils have been defined, by the Christian philosopher Marilyn McCord Adams as "evils in the participation in (the doing or suffering of) which gives one reason *prima facie* to doubt whether one's life could (given their inclusion in it) be a great good one on the whole".[3] At least this can seem the case for Western spectators of tragic events.

In the face of one such "horrendous evil" which killed around 230,000 men, women, and children, the Haiti earthquake event of January 2010, the publicly avowed atheist Richard Dawkins, in the *Washington Post*'s Faith Blog, railed against "the hypocrisy of Christian theology".[4] On the other hand, of the numerous survivors of earthquake and cholera I worked among during 2010–2011, and of the 150 or so survivors that I interviewed in the field research in Haiti in 2013 and 2014,

---

[3] I admit that I do find McCord Adams' focus upon the uniqueness of the Christian response to horrendous evils attractive, namely that it is the Christian faith that offers not just a balancing off, but also a final defeat of horrendous evil through the assurance of God's presence that overwhelms even the horrendous nature of what survivors have experienced. See Marilyn McCord Adams and Stewart Sutherland (1989) "Horrendous evils and the goodness of God", *Proceedings of the Aristotelian Society, Supplementary Volumes*, Vol. 63, pp. 297–323 (299).
[4] See Daniel Florien, "Dawkins on Haiti and the hypocrisy of Christian theology", *Patheos*: https://www.patheos.com/blogs/unreasonablefaith /2010/01/dawkins-on-haiti-and-the-hypocrisy-of-christian-theology / (last viewed 2 February 2018).

only two expressed any remote long-term distrust in God; all of them had survived terrifying experiences. Even one of those two admitted he had prayed when the shaking took place, and when his hotel threatened to collapse on him. God-talk remained irrepressible in the earthquake, even for atheists!

I found from my research quite a distinction between the effects disasters have upon actual survivors and the effects upon spectators who are geographically removed from the location. For the spectators of such disasters, all too often, the tragic events can turn hearts and minds to question how good God is when it comes to the worst moments in life, yet this was an effect not at all consistent with the experience of most, or even all, survivors I have listened to.[5]

Deliberately provocative, the title of this chapter (and book) gives a clue to where we shall travel. I respond to two questions: what is God's goodness? Then, what good does that goodness do for people caught up in disasters? Therefore, I propose, briefly, to reflect theologically upon the attribute of divine goodness from within the Christian tradition I embrace. Then I will proffer perspectives on the usefulness of that goodness, from the narrative testimonies of my research participants from three major catastrophes. In descending chronological order these events are: Typhoon Haiyan (Yolanda) in the Philippines (2013); the Haiti earthquake (2010); and Hurricane Katrina, New Orleans, USA (2005).

## What is God's goodness?

In Christian theology, speaking of God as good refers to his *ontological* goodness and to his *beneficent* goodness.

---

[5] See Roger Philip Abbott (2019), "'I will show you my faith by my human works': Addressing the nexus between philosophical theodicy and human suffering and loss in contexts of 'natural' disaster", *Religions*, Vol. 10, p. 213. DOI: 10.3390/rel10030213

God is *ontologically* good. God is good, just as he is love and righteousness. Stating that God *is* good, however, is not because there are laws independent of God for making such a judgment (the so-called "guided will theory"), and certainly not because humans say he is good, for that would make out humans to be God. The being of God defines the good, not some external criteria, and certainly not us. In Christian theology, being created in the image of God (Genesis 1:26–27) means that to be good has no other ultimate reference point than God himself. Our goodness is derived from our good Creator, or, as Thomas Aquinas stated, "But God is good through His essence, whereas all other things are good by participation". We, as humans, cannot rightly adjudicate when God is good; God tells us, and he shows us by his actions and by his demands. As Aquinas goes on to state: "Nothing, then, will be called good except in so far as it has a certain likeness of the divine goodness".[6] The good is God's self-approval. As my late New Testament professor, Donald Guthrie, stated, "the character of God is such that it is itself the standard that should determine all human notions of goodness".[7]

Therefore, when a man approached Jesus to inquire of him what good deed Jesus would say that he needed to do to gain eternal life, Jesus replied, with both a teasing and challenging question, to a man who thought of him as no more than a "good teacher", "Why do you call me good? No one is good except God alone" (Luke 18:18–19, ESV).

Theologically at least, we cannot say from one aspect of God (e.g. that God heals) that he is good, and from another aspect (e.g. that suffering occurs), that he is bad. We are not the judges of God because we are not adequate judges of what constitutes the good. In the words of Professor Nicholas Wolterstorff, which he penned following the death of his son, Eric, in a mountain-

---

[6] Thomas Aquinas, *Summa Contra Gentiles* (1259–1265), Book 1, chapter 40.

[7] Donald Guthrie, *New Testament Theology* (Leicester, UK: Inter-Varsity Press, 1981), p. 108.

climbing accident, "our net of meaning is too small".[8] That we are not adequate is self-evident from the history of human cruelty, and from the history of disasters in particular, which a burgeoning research is concluding are probably never natural but are tied to human evil (see the first two chapters of this book, for instance; also Abbott and White's *Narratives of Faith from the Haiti Earthquake*). God alone is good and sovereignly so. Therefore, by virtue of his ontology, God is never bad. Unlike some other deities, or the ontological dualism some like to see between the God of the Old Testament and the God of the New Testament, there is no Jekyll and Hyde personality in God! The ontological stability of God is something Christians have often found to be their only hope at times of disaster. Hence, they have spoken of God as their "Rock" (see Psalm 18:2, 31, 46).

The Apostle James draws on the astronomical phenomenon of planetary movements when he assures us that God is good because he is the "Father of lights, with whom there is no variation or shadow due to change" (James 1:17). As the Catholic theologian Thomas Weinandy has affirmed, "I believe that the singular passion of God's love, compassion, mercy, forgiveness, anger, etc., as witnessed in the Hebrew Scriptures, demands that his passionate love, compassion, mercy, forgiveness, anger, etc., be that of Wholly Other, for these passions themselves arise out of and testify to his total otherness".[9] This quote may be seen by some today as ironic in view of Weinandy's defence of the impassibility of God, an orthodox doctrine that has come under increasing criticism from those defending the passibility of God, a doctrine now viewed as being more favourable to addressing suffering and evil. Weinandy protests the opposite is true. I agree with him in this belief. These aspects of divine goodness do not change, thus challenging those who believe a passible God must be a more compassionate, humane God, a better ontology for God.

---

[8] Nicholas Wolterstorff, *Lament for a Son* (Grand Rapids, MI: Eerdmans, 1987), p. 74.

[9] Thomas G. Weinandy, *Does God Suffer?* (Edinburgh, UK: T&T Clark, 2000), p. 62.

Christian theologians also speak of God's *beneficent* goodness. That means God is good in terms of the benefits/goods he bestows upon us, his creatures, by virtue of his actions, which are driven by his goodness (Genesis 1:31). Because of his ontological goodness God has no wants or needs; but he does have a great disposition to give, to provide, and to care (James 1:17). As the late Oxford professor of literature, C. S. Lewis, stated, when reflecting on the problem of pain: "God is goodness. He can give good, but he cannot need or get it. In that sense all His love is, as it were, bottomlessly selfless by very definition. It has everything to give and nothing to receive".[10]

## What is God's goodness in respect to disasters?

These two aspects about the goodness of God – his ontological and his beneficent goodness – warrant three important caveats.

First, and most controversially, despite the fact of there being, on a global scale, so many disasters (and the science suggests they are likely to increase in number and in strength under the impact of climate change), for most of the spectators of disasters life abounds with more goodness than bad.[11] Even my sick cholera patients in Haiti, who had already survived a devastating earthquake, informed me of this in their prayers and praises. As sociologist Frank Ferudi points out, a too-inflated disaster consciousness, a common culturally conditioned phenomenon today in the Western world, runs the danger of over-exaggerating the severity and frequency of disasters.[12] When disasters strike, it can be easy to see life as one continuous disaster. (If anyone on

[10] C. S. Lewis, *The Problem of Pain* (London: Fount, 1940), p. 40, © 1940 CS Lewis pte Ltd. Used with permission.

[11] See Frank Ferudi (2007), "The changing meaning of disaster", *Area*, Vol. 39, Iss. 4, pp. 482–89, where he alerts readers to the way culture can define a disaster. He refers to the popular idea that the 1980s were the "decade of disasters", when in actual fact during the single year of 1952 there was a larger number of casualties than during the whole decade of the 1980s.

[12] Ferudi, p. 486.

Earth had reason to think like this, then my Haitian research participants did. Some did, but many did not.) This can lead us to overlook the predominance of the good in our lives. Another way of looking at it is to suggest that because of the preponderance of the good in life we can wrongly assume that we have a right to be spared the suffering and pain, and that a good God must be not only omnipotent and omniscient, but also be a "pleasure-maximiser".[13] For this reason, we can be all too easily inclined to rail at God when things seem to go wrong, but we find it equally easy to find some alternative explanation, often closer to our own achievements, for when things go right; and things do go right for a lot of us, a lot of the time. This fact was why the Apostle Paul could say to the crowds at Lystra – when he wanted to differentiate himself and Silas, as mere human beings, from the living God – that God "did not leave himself without witness, for *he did good* by giving you rains from heaven and fruitful seasons, satisfying your hearts with food and gladness" (Acts 14:17, ESV, emphasis mine).

One of the most notable forms of good that disasters evoke is the flood of human compassion, love, and practical goodness that envelopes the affected people, a factor that brought joy to participants in all of my disaster locations. For all the human flaws that bedevil disaster response today – and, my word, there are very many – these are contexts where the goodness of human nature, and therefore from the goodness of our Creator God, comes to the fore far more than the bad does. In her compelling book, *A Paradise Built in Hell*, the award-winning writer Rebecca Solnit insists that beliefs matter. Reflecting upon major disasters that happened between 1906–2005, she bucks the trend of typical disasters-reporting negativity by focusing upon actions and programmes of immense human compassion and care. These vignettes illustrate her belief that the common media reportage, and their readers' perception, that human subjects of disasters are selfish, weak, and panicked have little truth in them, Rather, something very different and surprising is true, namely:

---

[13] Adams and Sutherland, "Horrendous evils", p. 298.

When all the ordinary divides and patterns are shattered, people step up – not all, but the great preponderance – to become their brothers' keepers. And that purposefulness and connectedness bring joy even amid death, chaos, fear, and loss… Beliefs matter. And so do the facts behind them. The astonishing gaps between common beliefs and actualities about disaster behaviour limits the possibilities, and changing beliefs could fundamentally change much more. Horrible in itself, disaster is sometimes a door back into paradise.[14]

Indeed, many of the survivors I interviewed told me the disaster highlighted both the best and the worst about humans, but only the best about God.

When we ask, "what good is God?" we also mean what use is he? Therefore, another important caveat from the beneficent goodness of God we should remember is that God's beneficence is not a resource we can just snatch out of his hands into ours. Christian theology does not teach that God should be "used", as some utility for maximizing our safety and pleasure, as if his beneficence is a commodity we can dip into just when we need it most, and ignore when we no longer feel the need. Again, C. S. Lewis put such ingratitude most starkly when he wrote, "We regard God as an airman regards his parachute. It is there for emergencies but he hopes he'll never have to use it".[15] God's beneficent goodness is not a parachute or a divine paramedic's bag; though, even as I say this, how many of us have known experiences of just crying out to God for help in an emergency, and receiving it, even when we had no serious regard for God either before the crisis or when life settled down afterwards?

The proof of divine goodness is measured in Christian theology, not by answering *Why* did God allow such and such

---

[14] Rebecca Solnit, *A Paradise Built in Hell: The Extraordinary Communities that Arise in Disaster* (New York: Penguin, 2009), p. 3.
[15] Lewis, *The Problem of Pain,* p. 76, © 1940 CS Lewis pte Ltd. Used with permission.

to happen, but by *What* has God done to address the problem? Christian theology is clear that God's goodness is evidenced in God's self-giving, generous actions and, supremely, in the gift to us of his Son – "In this the love of God was made manifest among us, that God sent his only Son into the world, so that we might live through him" – and such love becomes the mainspring for the love with which Christians respond to others: "Beloved, if God so loved us, we also ought to love one another" (1 John 4:9, 11, ESV). The Apostle Paul drove home his exhortations to Christians to show self-denying compassion, by drawing upon the Trinitarian perichoresis (deference of the Persons) in the incarnation of Christ (Philippians 2:1–4; see also verses 5–9).

Therefore, in the context of disasters, Christian theology affirms that God's best resources for us are activated in Christ, and Christ's actions are to be incarnated today in Christians' responses to disasters. In the words of the nineteenth-century Princeton theologian, B. B. Warfield:

> He [Christ] took no account of self. He was not led by His divine impulse out of the world, driven back into the recesses of His own soul to brood morbidly over his own needs, until to gain His own seemed worth all sacrifice to Him. He was led by His love for others into the world, to forget himself in the needs of others, to sacrifice self once and for all upon the altar of sympathy. Self-sacrifice brought Christ into the world. And self-sacrifice will lead us, His followers, not away but into the midst of men [people]. Whenever [people] suffer, there will we be to comfort.[16]

In the Christian tradition, this good God is the ultimate emergency planner, and responder, in fact, because, as Cornelius Plantinga

---

[16] Benjamin Breckinridge Warfield, "Imitating the incarnation" in Samuel Craig (ed.), *The Person and Work of Christ* (Edinburgh, UK: P & R, 1970), p. 574. Used with permission from P&R Publishing Co. P O Box 817, Phillipsburg, N J 08865  www.prpbooks.com

Jr. says, "sin is the longest running of human emergencies",[17] for which God alone, at great pains to himself, has provided the remedy and recovery in his Son (Ephesians 1:7–10).

A third and final caveat is that the goodness of God, in this temporal world, does not mean that distressing things cannot, will not, or should not happen. For example, as Moo and White have already highlighted in their respective chapters in this book, we must not equate the wild – and risky – features of God's good creation with evil. God's good creation includes the wild and the untamed (Job 39, 41) together with the potential risks they pose, but not the evil. However, the ontological and beneficent goodness of God, operating in both a temporal and probationary world, allows for the possibility of evil and tragedy, but such realities are not ontologies created by God, nor are they eternal; but they will be justly and finally resolved in God's *good* justice and grace. It is this assurance of hope that is so very good to those whose foundations of life have been shattered traumatically by a disaster. However, even during this life, as Marilyn Adams reminds us:

> Horrendous evils can be overcome only by the goodness of God. Relative to human nature, participation in horrendous evils and loving intimacy with God are alike disproportionate: for the former threatens to engulf the good in an individual human life with evil, while the latter guarantees the reverse engulfment of evil by good… Because intimacy with God so outscales relations (good or bad) with any creatures, integration into the human person's relationship with God confers significant meaning and positive value even on horrendous suffering. This result coheres with basic Christian intuition, that the powers of darkness are stronger than humans, but they are no match for God![18]

---

[17] Plantinga Jr., *Not the Way it's Supposed to be*, p. 5.
[18] Adams and Sutherland, "Horrendous evils", p. 309.

Taking this theological perspective on the goodness of God, how does it hold up against the experience of survivors of some of the worst disasters in contemporary history? What narrative evidence do these primary sources present for us?

## Bantayan Island, Philippines

My first witness is the pastor of Bantayan Baptist Church on Bantayan Island, a small island off the north-western tip of the larger island of Cebu, Philippines. Dennis came to live on Bantayan Island when he was just five years old. He always dreamed of becoming an engineer, but in fact became a church pastor instead.

Dennis got warning of an approaching typhoon some five days before it struck. He held special meetings in his three churches to explain how serious the coming storm was likely to be and told his congregants to prepare adequately. This meant stocking up with food, flashlights, medicines, and first-aid materials. He also advised members to evacuate from their own homes into his church, which was a designated evacuation centre.

On the morning of 8 November 2013, Dennis woke up at around 4 a.m. to pray and read his Bible. At 7 a.m., he, his wife, and their two children ate breakfast together. By 8 a.m., the skies became darker and the wind increased, and the family decided to move inside the church. The typhoon struck first from the east, with strong force, and then after an hour or so it stopped (see Figure 3.1).

When the family went outside, they saw that their own house, adjoining the church, had no roof left on it. Yet the weather was bright and clear! A neighbour explained that they were in the eye of the storm and that they needed to go back inside the church again. Sure enough, the skies soon darkened as the typhoon struck again, this time from the west. The winds were much stronger, and the rain lashed down, making visibility almost impossible. Inside the church someone stood against the door, which the winds were threatening to blow open; Dennis stood against a concrete wall that was throbbing under the wind pressure. After the first wind, they had removed the jalousies (folding glass sections) from the windows, allowing the stronger winds to blow through them, rather than burst them and turn glass shards into lethal missiles.

When Pastor Dennis surveyed his premises after the typhoon, he saw so much material devastation – to his church, to his house, and to his adjoining school. Here is his reflection of what happened after that survey:

> Right after the typhoon I was so down because those classrooms that were there before the typhoon... I loaned [borrowed money] to have [them]. And I am not finished paying [for] it. So one evening I was sitting outside... talking to God; I said, "Lord, I think the school is done; I am done; I have no classroom. I think I [will] just finish the school year [in] March and then... close the school. Because how can I build? I'm still paying for my loan. So, no more". And then I ask[ed] him, "If you allow me to continue in this ministry, please bring someone".

One week later, at around 5 a.m., as Dennis sat inside the church building that had become their temporary home, he was praying again, "Lord, if you want me to continue this school, and the church ministry, please bring someone here to help me".

Around 5:30 a.m., three foreigners opened the gate into his compound. They explained to Dennis that they had planned to visit some other parts of the Philippines that the typhoon had struck, but they feared the looting going on there. So they were directed to the island of Cebu and then to Bantayan Island. They had arrived onto the island in their van, via the ferry crossing, at around 4:30 a.m. that morning, and they had prayed, "Lord, make us a blessing to this island; bring us into a Baptist church". Not knowing anyone or having any contacts, they just drove, looking for a Baptist church.

They shared their aid with the group in Dennis' church, and a friendship developed between them, so that they remained with the church – helping rebuild the premises and from there reaching out to others around the island, and then, as time went on, introducing self-sustainable livelihood projects.

For Dennis and his church members, their faith held strong, and held even stronger following their experience of the strongest typhoon ever to make landfall.

## Haiti

It is important to understand that the tragic influences upon a disaster survivor's life are not limited to those brought about by the major disaster. A survivor's resilience is often affected by events that occur either before or after such disasters. Helena's experience is a case in point.

High up in the mountains behind a Haitian town, 30 miles (50 km) or so from the capital, Port-au-Prince, we conducted interviews at a medical centre. One young lady, Helena, came accompanied by her 21-month-old son; they had come to see the doctor and Helena had volunteered for interview. She told me that she had been born and raised in that village. They were a family that survived off growing their own crops on the steep sides of the mountains where they lived.

At the time of the earthquake in January 2010, Helena was lodging down in the main town as she was attending high school there. While looking after her neighbour's four-year-old child, suddenly the earthquake shook the house and the house began falling down. She and the child managed to escape the property without harm. To look for relatives and friends, she went around the local hospitals where she saw people who had lost body parts, a woman with her belly cut in half and her intestines hanging out, and all manner of other gruesome sights. The sounds and sights of what she witnessed that day as a young woman still reduced her to tears when she recalled the memories to me three years later.

After the earthquake, Helena spent eight days living in a tent on a temporary campsite in the town, where she found everyone shared what they had with each other. However, before long she became weak and sick because of the trauma and from the poor food. As a churchgoing Christian, she explained to me that after the earthquake she understood God better, as a Creator, and that, on the other hand, when she looked at humans, she realized we could all die in the blink of an eye.

While at school, before the earthquake, she was in a relationship with a man she liked at the time. As the months rolled on, they saw less and less of each other, as he had moved away to the capital city. One day, some months after the earthquake, while Helena was on a bus travelling to Port-au-Prince to meet her brother, she received a call from the boyfriend, who was jealous about her not seeing him so often. In the end, he wore Helena down with his pleas for her to visit him, even offering to meet her bus to collect her and bring her to his house. In the end, she relented. Once back in his house, he asked her to move and live there with him, telling her she would if she really loved him. When Helena declined, he raped her. She became pregnant, and when she later announced this to him, he demanded that she abort the child. She refused, telling him she would rather die with the child than have an abortion, whereupon he wanted nothing more to do with her. Helena returned to her home in the mountains. She felt unable to speak to her church pastor, and so ashamed and isolated in her community that she started to attend a different church outside the area.

Helena went on to bear her child, and that was he with her on the day of our interview. It was clear to me at our first interview that this young mother was finding life very hard to bear. Afterwards, I asked her if it was the earthquake she felt more depressed by or the rape. She said it was the rape, as she had not spoken to anyone about it since it had happened. With my pastoral "hat" on, and in accord with our approved ethics protocol, I gave her the opportunity to talk in another session a few days after our research interview. We arranged to meet again at the medical centre, on which occasion she shared with me more about the rape incident. After she had finished telling me her tragic story, I applauded her for what I saw as being an incredible act of courage on her part in her agreeing to become a mother to the child. I sought to reassure her that it was she who had been violated. When I visited the village a year later, we met again and I found a very different woman. She was smiling and much more alive.

Helena told me that shortly after our previous conversation she had plucked up the courage to speak to her pastor and rather than reacting with the anger or revulsion she had so feared, he was gracious and accepting, and assured her there was no risk of her being isolated out of the church. She found the church members too embraced her and her child, as did her natural siblings and parents. Like Dennis on Bantayan Island, Helena effused thanks to God and spoke of how it was only her faith, and the support of other Christians, that brought her through that double tragedy of earthquake and rape. For Helena the goodness of God was manifested to her in terms of the compassionate care response and support she experienced from her local church following her revelation to her pastor of the rape incident, and the way this emboldended her return to raise her child and to feel secure again in the local community. Her church acceptance now figured more strongly in her life than did the shame brought upon her by the rape.

## New Orleans, Louisiana, USA

Down on Tennessee Street, in the Lower Ninth Ward, at 10 a.m. on a Sunday morning in 2005, a day before Hurricane Katrina skirted the city of New Orleans, 50-year-old Richard had packed the car. He was making ready to evacuate himself, his 73-year-old mother, his 60-year-old cousin with learning difficulties, his 45-year-old brother, and his three grandchildren, aged two, three, and four respectively. They hit the road to drive out of town toward Baton Rouge, heading for Nashville, Tennessee, but it soon became clear that Richard's mother was too sick from her Parkinson's disease and a heart condition to endure the journey. Instead, they headed for the Superdome, New Orleans' designated "shelter of last resort". At the Superdome, they had to stand in queues while they awaited clearance for entering, and it soon became obvious that Richard's mother was too sick to stand in a queue in the searing hot Sun for any length of time. The Superdome was meant to be set up to include people with special needs, but the authorities were not yet ready, and so the family were told to come back later.

Importantly, in view of a commonly held view that people who stayed behind were foolish, this family had done everything they had been told to do by way of evacuating their home and seeking safe refuge, but their compliance with the system had not worked.

By this time, Richard's adult sons were driving the only cars they had out of town, and the floodgates had closed behind them, effectively sealing Richard and the remaining family members inside the city. They returned to their home to wait out the storm, just as they had done for many previous storms.

Around 4 a.m., Monday morning, Richard's brother woke him up to say they had water in the house. Soon the water was increasing in depth at an alarming rate, and family members were floating on bits of furniture. They dragged a china cupboard to use as a ladder to climb up into the attic. One by one, they all managed to climb up into the attic, where the brother kicked out a vent to allow them to climb out onto the roof, if the water kept on rising.

The floodwater continued to pour in, and with such massive force and depth that it lifted the wooden house off its foundation altogether and began to drag it and the occupants away at a speed of 10–15 mph. As the house broke up, Richard brought his three-year-old granddaughter onto the roof first. Turning around to get the other two children, unbeknown to him, the three-year-old child slipped off the roof into 25 ft of water. The remainder of the group then clambered up onto the roof. The four-year-old jumped into the water to try to rescue her young sister. Failing to find the sister, she swam to a truck that was floating nearby. At one stage, the truck flowed near to the roof section and she was able to jump from the truck back onto the roof. Next, the cousin fell into the water, and they managed to pull him out, but he fell back in, and they managed to haul him back onto the roof again. Distressed about her nephew's plight, this was just when the mother's Parkinson's kicked back in again and shook her out of Richard's hand and she fell into the raging floodwater. They managed to pull her back onto the roof, but she fell back under the water a second, and then a third time, by which time she had stopped breathing. The group, together with a neighbouring family that had clambered aboard the roof from their own waterborne home, stayed on that roof for seven hours before being rescued by another resident with his boat.

The effect of this experience upon Richard was huge – especially the loss of his granddaughter and his mother. They had had to leave the mother's body on the roof of the house when they were rescued. A hundred and twenty days later, her body was found by the family. They had given up waiting for the authorities to search for her and had come and searched for her themselves. They also found the granddaughter's body. (Figure 3.2 shows a section of the area after the floodwaters subsided.)

This is just a small vignette of Richard's whole story. When I asked him how it had all affected him, he told me:

Well, it affected me to the point where I had to go back to my faith [he was raised as a Lutheran]. And what I mean by that is, if you believe – and notice I said *if* – *if* you believe in God's grace, *if* you believe in God's will; basically, I had to take those *if*s out and just trust it, you know what I'm saying? Because what I used to do, I used to sing a song "My Baby's Gone" (and I'm crying my ass off). When I changed that song to "My Baby's Gone *Home*" it changed the whole complexion. So I can live in misery or I can open up myself to the grace that he [God] has for us.

Again, it was his faith that came into its own in Richard's worst moments. He never spoke of blaming God.

In conclusion, in each of my research projects I have told participants that I would be a voice *for them*, not for myself. These are people who had endured the most horrendous evils, and yet still believed that God is good and that God has been a great good for them in their experience. They deserve to be listened to far more seriously than as mere spectators of disasters. I speak for them in answer to the question raised in this chapter: What good is God? They each reply, "Very good! We could not have coped without him".

# CHAPTER 4

# PHYSICIAN HEAL THYSELF: HIS GRACE IS SUFFICIENT

## LINDA MOBULA

I have responded to multiple humanitarian emergencies and witnessed the suffering of myriad individuals in multiple settings. Whether it be in the context of a large-scale outbreak, on the inpatient medicine wards, intensive care units, or after a natural disaster. As a physician I have seen suffering in the form of the loss of a family member or in the immense physical suffering from a complex illness. I have had to comfort many families in the face of a great loss. One of my most poignant memories as a doctor was sharing a life-threatening diagnosis with a patient. He was the sole caregiver for his wife who was a double amputee. I watched him slowly deteriorate and become a shadow of himself as his cancer metastasized. The last time I visited him in his home, he had lost more than 100 lb (45 kg) and was extremely weak. It was not long after this that his wife called me to inform me of his death. However, it wasn't until the West Africa Ebola outbreak that I truly comprehended the meaning of the sufficiency of God's grace and how much I truly needed to rely on God to be my strength when I was weak and surrounded by suffering. As it says in 2 Corinthians 12:9–10 (NIV):

> "My grace is sufficient for you, for my power is made perfect in weakness". Therefore, I will boast all the more gladly about my weaknesses, so that Christ's power may rest on me. That is why, for Christ's sake, I delight in weaknesses, in insults, in hardships, in persecutions, in difficulties. For when I am weak, then I am strong.

I hope that my following stories will show that weakness and suffering are gateways through which God works in and through us.

## Suffering and grace during the Ebola response

I was deployed to Monrovia, Liberia in July 2014 to work at the Eternal Life Winning Africa (ELWA-2) Ebola Treatment Centre. It was the first outbreak of Ebola virus disease (EVD) arising in multiple countries in West Africa. Previous outbreaks of Ebola were relatively small and limited to rural areas in Central and Eastern Africa. The first known outbreak of Ebola virus disease occurred in 1976, in what was then called Zaire, now known as the Democratic Republic of the Congo. Ebola was discovered during the 1976 outbreak by a group of scientists who were part of the Ministry of Health, along with several international universities. Until 2014, EVD was known to kill up to 90 per cent of infected individuals.

At the end of July 2014, I was in the courtyard of the only Ebola Treatment Centre in Monrovia when a young Liberian mother approached me. Her son was being treated for Ebola, and she pleaded with me, "Please save Solomon, my son, he is my only son". She then looked up to the sky, with her hands lifted toward the heavens, and prayed in a loud voice asking God to heal her son. I reassured her that we would care for her son to the best of our ability. As I started my rounds the next morning, I learned that Solomon had died in the middle of the night. I could barely contain my own tears when imagining his mother's devastation. I could not understand why her son did not survive, especially since she had asked God to heal him. She seemed to have faith that her son would survive. Wasn't that enough?

It was only a few days after Solomon's death that a family of six were admitted to the ELWA, and one after the next, they all died. Once again, I questioned where God was during those difficult moments. How could he let vulnerable individuals suffer from a devastating illness that robs them of their dignity and their life? I questioned God over and over again during the course of those few weeks as the Ebola Treatment Centre flooded with patients. I was also frustrated with the international community which at the time had limited interest in a disease that was so far from home.

My friend and colleague, Dr Kent Brantly, was one of the only American physicians treating Ebola patients at that time. Suddenly, he contracted the same disease that he had been called to treat. I felt paralyzed as I watched Dr Brantly and others suffer. Many people died despite aggressive hydration and supportive care. Some people died because of the tyranny of the disease but others died because they accessed care too late. Communities and individuals considered admission to an Ebola Treatment Centre to be a death sentence, which only compounded their fears and caused delays. When health care providers who worked alongside Dr Brantly discovered he had contracted EVD, they began to question whether Personal Protective Equipment (PPE) was effective, and as a result they stopped providing care due to fear of exposure and death.

On 31 July 2014, I received a call from Dr Brantly who had begun to deteriorate rapidly. Based on my clinical assessment and the overwhelming mortality rate, I did not believe he would survive that night. When he fell ill, there had been discussions with the National Institutes of Health about using an experimental therapy, ZMapp, a cocktail of monoclonal antibodies. The drug was originally being considered to treat Dr Sheik Umar Khan, a researcher who had worked on viral hemorrhagic fevers. His team of physicians decided not to administer the drug, and, unfortunately, he died shortly after. It is not clear whether Dr Khan would have survived if he had received the treatment. However, the precious dose was shipped to Liberia. As there was only one dose available, Dr Brantly had graciously agreed to let Nancy Writebol, a missionary, receive the treatment. However, because Kent was deteriorating so rapidly, we decided that he should receive it.

I prayed as I prepared to administer the treatment. I understood the principles of science and the evidence of the effectiveness of ZMapp in non-human primates, and I recognized that more than science was needed. The experimental treatment had never been administered to a human before, but Dr Brantly's situation was so dire. Even though I did my due diligence and read the papers that studied its efficacy, I found that there was no comparable alternative therapy available. Understanding science is critical, but faith that those principles will work is also essential to science. And so that led me to pray for Dr Brantly as I administered the investigational drug. Despite having a keen understanding of how this drug could potentially cause harm, my colleagues and I were nonetheless willing to take the chance.

To do no harm is both an ethical principle and a humanitarian principle. Abuse of vulnerable persons under the auspices of research has been documented throughout history. When mortality rates are extremely high and there is no proven treatment for a disease, this principle may be considered in order to ensure that lives are saved. However, this is never an easy decision as harm can inevitably occur.

The 2013–2016 West Africa Ebola outbreak caused more than 11,000 deaths, greater than the number of casualties in all prior historical Ebola outbreaks.[1] The non-governmental organization (NGO) Samaritan's Purse worked alongside *Médecins Sans Frontières*, managing the only functional Ebola Treatment Centre in Monrovia. Prior to the World Health Organization's declaration of a public health emergency of international concern (PHEIC) on 6 August 2014, I worked with a small group of brave individuals striving to ensure that patients suffering from this deadly illness received proper medical care. Simultaneously, frightened community members bearing machetes approached the Ebola Treatment Centre, driven by fear, rumours, and uncertainty.

---

[1] *Ebola Outbreak 2014–2016,* World Health Organization: https://www. who.int/csr/disease/ebola/en/ (last viewed 21 January 2020).

In Monrovia, we were receiving more and more patients from counties outside Montserrado County, but did not have sufficient bed capacity to accommodate these patients. It is particularly challenging to respond to a surge of Ebola patients, as it requires more staff and physical infrastructure that adhere to careful infection prevention and control (IPC) measures. In contrast to responding to cholera outbreaks, in an Ebola Treatment Centre all staff must don PPE to care for patients, which limits the amount of time one can spend with a patient. I was becoming more overwhelmed as the outbreak spun out of control. I feared for the wellbeing of our personnel and worried about our ability to care for patients with limited staff.

I had never felt so powerless as a physician. I personally experienced heartbreak and uncertainty as more patients died each day. I had difficulties reconciling a good God with what I was witnessing – the Bible states that God is good, and yet he seemed to be silent. In fact, he seemed absent over the course of the three years of the outbreak. How can God be good when he lets the most vulnerable suffer?

It was 2 a.m. on 1 August 2014 in Monrovia, Liberia, and I had just administered the first dose of ZMapp to Dr Brantly. As I sat next to his bed, donned in PPE, I watched him pick up his Intravenous Line, get out of bed and walk to the bathroom. He had almost died hours prior, yet I had just witnessed a complete miracle – science and faith working together in a way I had never experienced before (see Figure 4.1). I came to the conclusion that as a human being I was not self-sufficient and I needed to completely rely on God's grace.

Grace is often defined as unmerited mercy, which nobody deserves in their own right. Mother Teresa once wrote:

> I don't think there is anyone who needs God's help and grace as much as I do. Sometimes I feel so helpless and weak. I think that is why God uses me. Because I cannot depend on my own strength, I rely on Him twenty-four hours a day. If

the day had even more hours, then I would need His help and grace during those as well.[2]

The weaker we are, the stronger God's grace is in our lives. *The Message* paraphrase of the Bible translates 2 Corinthians 12:9–10 as:

It was a case of Christ's strength moving in on my weakness. Now I take my limitations in stride, and with good cheer, these limitations that cut me down to size – abuse, accidents, opposition, bad breaks. I just let Christ take over! And so the weaker I get, the stronger I become.

I was deployed to Guinea, the country where the first index case for the West Africa outbreak was identified, as I continued to struggle to understand the sufficiency of God's grace. I was attending a focus group discussion with Ebola survivors in the Forest Region of Guinea. A Guinean mother recounted how she carried her child on her back while she walked for hours, attempting to find an Ebola Treatment Centre so her child would survive. However, her child died on her back and she herself began to develop symptoms. We were able to treat her, and she ultimately survived, but her husband later threw her out of the house because he did not want to deal with the stigma of having a wife that was an "Ebola survivor".

How did I ultimately reconcile these issues? In 2015, I had the opportunity to return to Liberia and visit what remained of the ELWA-2 in Monrovia. The following words were written by a patient suffering from Ebola on a wall inside ELWA-2: "God is with us in here" (see Figure 4.2). Despite the immense suffering Ebola patients encountered, they were able to still feel God's presence in the midst of darkness and pain. I also recalled that

---

[2] Mother Teresa, *The Power of Prayer* (New York: MJF Books, 1998), p. 3, taken from United States Catholic Catechism for Adults (USCCB, 2006), pp. 479–80.

the year before I had even heard an Ebola patient sing hymns. "You will keep in perfect peace those whose minds are steadfast, because they trust in you" (Isaiah 26:3, NIV).

## Suffering, grace, and disasters: Haiti and the Philippines

There had been many other instances where I didn't understand why the innocent suffered. In October 2010, I was in Cité Soleil, Haiti's largest slum, treating cholera patients. On 12 January 2010, Haiti had experienced a magnitude 7.0 earthquake that devastated Haiti and caused an estimated 230,000 deaths. This was followed by a cholera outbreak that had been introduced by Nepalese United Nations (UN) soldiers, who had come to provide assistance. "The perfect storm", it was called. From October 2010 to 31 December 2012, the number of cholera cases exceeded 635,000, of which around 350,000 (55 per cent) were hospitalized and almost 8,000 died. Haiti had not experienced a cholera outbreak for more than 200 years.

I will not ever forget this young girl who was brought in by her mother. "*Bwe, bwe*", she cried out in Creole, which means "drink, drink". I looked down at her three-year-old body, weak from dehydration, her face, eyes sunken and lifeless, the "face of cholera". Quickly filling, dispensing, and refilling my syringe of oral rehydration solution I tried to meet her every request for "*bwe, bwe*". I looked around the room, a sea of silent children, who also had cholera, were lying on cots receiving hydration that was saving their lives.

In post-earthquake Haiti, I met a wonderful family that lived in an Internally Displaced Persons (IDP) camp outside of Port-au-Prince. The mother had five children, one of whom had been sexually assaulted, and a son who was progressively becoming blind. Her son was legally blind with Keratitis, a condition that he had likely acquired from vitamin A deficiency or from a parasitic infection. He was a very kind child, who constantly wanted to help his mother. They lived in a tent, located in the middle of a sea of thousands of other tents. Despite living in extreme poverty, the mother once offered me a precious gift of avocadoes which, I am sure, was the only food they had. I refused to take away what was likely to be their only meal. She kept on insisting that I take the avocadoes, so I unwillingly did. I was struck by the generosity of this family, who despite their own losses gave generously.

I was involved in the response to Typhoon Haiyan a few years later with Samaritan's Purse. I travelled to the Philippines on 8 November 2013, just after the category 5 typhoon, with winds of 150 mph, struck the island of Leyte. My team sat in silence and utter disbelief as we journeyed from the airport to our hotel. Trees had fallen everywhere, homes were destroyed; in short, there was utter devastation. I provided medical care to families that were affected by the typhoon through mobile clinics and at the Schistosomiasis Research Hospital in Leyte. Over and over again, I heard horror stories of water filling homes, and families struggling to hang on for dear life. The local staff at the Schistosomiasis Research Hospital would come in each day to lovingly care for patients despite suffering their own trauma.

One day, I received an invitation to a church service, which took place on the porch of a pastor's home. I was amazed at how freely the congregation worshipped despite having suffered this immense tragedy. During the sermon, the pastor shared a personal and poignant story. As he and his family went without food for several days, one of his children asked what their attitude should be. He replied, "Son, though we don't have any food or water to drink, let's praise God because we are alive". I reflected on the mere sufficiency that God's grace represented for this family.

I encountered many individuals who suffered and one in particular brought tears to my eyes. I listened as a patient I was seeing described the insomnia she had been experiencing since Typhoon Haiyan. "I stay up all night", she said. "I keep on thinking about what happened the day the typhoon hit. I was positive I was going to die. I remember seeing the water rush into my house. I still have heart palpitations when I think about it". I could have simply written a prescription for a medication that would help with her anxiety as well as insomnia. However, in addition to providing medical care, I wanted to give her something else. I asked if I could read Psalm 91 with her and she nodded in agreement.

> He who dwells in the shelter of the Most High will abide in the shadow of the Almighty... You will not fear the terror of the night, nor the arrow that flies by day, nor the pestilence that stalks in darkness, nor the destruction that wastes at noonday.

I didn't realize how comforting those words (particularly verses 1, 5, and 6, ESV) could be for someone who had lost everything. As I continued to read the entire psalm, she began to sob. I thanked God that he spared her life and thanked him for the plan he had for her life. She gripped my hands forcefully and cried while I finished in prayer for her. "Thank you for coming", she said. Those four simple words greatly moved me. My public health background taught me about the importance of designing interventions to reach masses. "Saving lives, millions at a time" was the motto I often heard. On that particular day, reaching just one person was enough for me.

## Reflections on suffering

In Habakkuk 3:17–19 (NIV), the Bible says:

> Though the fig-tree does not bud and there are no grapes on the vines, though the olive crop fails and the fields produce no food, though there are no sheep in the sheepfold and no cattle in the stalls, yet I will rejoice in the LORD; I will be joyful in God my Saviour. The Sovereign LORD is my strength; he makes my feet like the feet of a deer; he enables me to tread on the heights.

In the Western world, the scope of the difficulties we encounter seem trivial in comparison to the loss of life, devastation, and suffering encountered in other parts of the world. We must be able to learn from the suffering our fellow brothers and sisters encounter during such disasters.

Though I do not fully understand the reason for human suffering, one fact remains: God does not always cause suffering. Sometimes, we as human beings do not treat our neighbours as we ought. For example, if there was less corruption and more investment in health systems, perhaps a deadly disease such as Ebola would not ravage communities in the way it has. I admit this cannot fully explain the reason for all suffering that occurs, but I have learned many lessons from suffering. God does not take away our pain or sorrows. He gives us our daily bread in order to strengthen us each day, so we can handle pain. Our job is to seek him during these challenging times and to allow him to awaken our faith in him. According to 2 Corinthians 1:5–6 (NIV):

> For just as we share abundantly in the sufferings of Christ, so also our comfort abounds through Christ. If we are distressed, it is for your comfort and salvation; if we are comforted, it is for your comfort, which produces in you patient endurance of the same sufferings we suffer.

Perhaps one of the objectives of suffering is to create and strengthen resilience, as well as patience and trust in our Creator. This seems to be an oxymoron, as in some modern church teachings, suffering is viewed as a curse. Ravi Zacharias states the following:

> God alone can weave a pattern from the disparate threads of our lives – whether suffering, success, joy, or heartache – and fashion a magnificent design. Perhaps today, if you will stop and reflect on it, you will see that the Father is seeking to weave a beautiful tapestry in your life.[3]

---

[3] Ravi Zacharias, *Just thinking*: https://www.rzim.org/read/just-thinking-magazine/think-again-2 (last viewed 22 September 2019).

In the midst of tragedy and suffering, what ought a Christian physician to do? King David said it well, in 1 Chronicles 28:20 (NIV):

> Be strong and courageous, and do the work. Do not be afraid or discouraged, for the LORD God, my God, is with you. He will not fail you or forsake you until all the work for the service of the temple of the LORD is finished.

Our call is to relieve suffering and provide compassionate care, as Jesus commanded us to do in the Gospel according to Matthew 25:35–40 (NIV):

> "For I was hungry and you gave me something to eat, I was thirsty and you gave me something to drink, I was a stranger and you invited me in, I needed clothes and you clothed me, I was sick and you looked after me, I was in prison and you came to visit me". Then the righteous will answer him, "Lord, when did we see you hungry and feed you, or thirsty and give you something to drink? When did we see you a stranger and invite you in, or needing clothes and clothe you? When did we see you ill or in prison and go to visit you?" The King will reply, "Truly I tell you, whatever you did for one of the least of these brothers and sisters of mine, you did for me".

## Humanitarian principles

The principle of humanity requires that all human beings deserve to be treated humanely and equally in all circumstances by saving lives, alleviating suffering, and ensuring respect for the individual. This principle stems from the Geneva Convention, which was born out of a movement created by Swiss banker Jean-Henri Dunant. Dunant won the Nobel Peace Prize for the creation of the International Committee of the Red Cross, after witnessing the aftermath of the battle of Solferino during a business trip.

Despite the lack of supplies and materials, he not only purchased his own but motivated volunteers to provide services to the wounded, irresepective of their side in the conflict, following the slogan *"Tutti fratelli"* (All are brothers).

## Compassion

"Compassion is a part of professional competence and is perhaps as important as technical competence, because both are required to effect meaningful healing".[4]

To act with "compassion" requires the following:

- Recognizing that your neighbour is suffering.
- Internal response.
- Relieving the suffering.[5]

The International Health Regulations, or IHR (2005), is a legal treaty agreement between 196 countries, including all World Health Organization Member States, to work together for global health security.[6] Through the IHR, countries have agreed to build their capacities to detect, assess, and report public health events. As part of this process, countries are obligated to report on surveillance of public health events. How does one reconcile reporting on the "number of cases", while continuing to maintain the humanity of these individuals? Each time I participated in

---

[4] G. L. Larkin, K. Iserson, Z. Kassutto, G. Freas, K. Delaney, J. Krimm, T. Schmidt, J. Simon, A. Calkins, J. Adams (2009) "Virtue in emergency medicine", Acad Emerg Med, Vol. 16, Iss. 1, pp. 51–55.

[5] R. A. Cameron, B. L. Mazer, J. M. DeLuca, S. G. Mohile, R. M. Epstein (2015) "In search of compassion: A new taxonomy of compassionate physician behaviours", Health Expect., Vol. 18, Iss. 5, pp. 1672–85. doi:10.1111/hex.12160

[6] *Strengthening Health Security by Implementing the International Health Regulations.* World Health Organization: https://www.who.int/ihr/en/ (last viewed 21 January 2020).

meetings at the Emergency Operations Centre in West Africa, I challenged myself to think of the "number of cases" as individuals, family members, and not just as "cases".

Sir William Osler, one of the fathers of Internal Medicine (the prevention, diagnosis, and treatment of adult diseases), has a famous quote:

> The good physician treats the disease; the great physician treats the patient who has the disease. Medicine is a science of uncertainty and an art of probability. One of the first duties of the physician is to educate the masses not to take medicine. We are here to add what we can to life, not to get what we can from life. The desire to take medicine is perhaps the greatest feature which distinguishes man from animals. The greater the ignorance the greater the dogmatism. The natural man has only two primal passions, to get and to beget. He who studies medicine without books sails an uncharted sea, but he who studies medicine without patients does not go to sea at all. Look wise, say nothing, and grunt. Speech was given to conceal thought. The best preparation for tomorrow is to do today's work superbly well.[7]

The practice of public health, which promotes and protects the health of populations, should also focus on gaining a better understanding of the communities who have the "disease" or "outbreak" one is trying to prevent. How is this possible if public health is focused on populations, rather than on an individual? In the case of outbreaks, one must consider a response to an outbreak that is affecting communities, rather than simply considering the outbreak alone. This is particularly relevant to the case of the 2018 Ebola outbreak in the Democratic Republic

---

[7] R. M. Centor (2007) "To be a great physician, you must understand the whole story", MedGenMed, Vol. 9, Iss. 1, p. 59. (Source: ACP press)

of the Congo. For the first time, an Ebola outbreak occurred in the setting of ongoing conflict, where several armed groups had been terrorizing and kidnapping the local population for more than twenty years. The Democratic Republic of Congo is a country where so many continue to suffer and experience extreme poverty, and where many women continue to experience gender-based violence. Social Science in Humanitarian Action Platform (SSHAP) is a group conducting social science research in the midst of the Ebola outbreak in North Kivu, in the eastern Democratic Republic of the Congo. They aided in setting up mechanisms that allowed responders to gather feedback from communities. One memorable and commonly expressed quote from the community was as follows: "First the kidnappings (2010–2014), then the massacres (2014 – present), now Ebola".[8] Combining humanity, medicine, and public health will definitely improve the quality of services rendered to the individuals we are called to serve as Christians. In addition, as physicians we have the moral obligation to improve our technical skills.

## Science and faith

Science and faith can complement each other. One must believe in the principles of science to provide medical care, and that the evidence that is generated through research supports our practice as a clinician. Belief in science does not preclude the belief that God can use physicians to heal, utilizing the principles of medicine and science. Sir William Osler describes medicine as an art of probability, which implies that though we apply certain principles of medicine and science, not everyone receives the same outcome. The same applies to prayer, as not everyone receives the answer they desire from God.

---

[8] R. Sweet and J. Bedford (2018) "WhatsApp and local media", Grand Nord, 9–18 September, Brief: UNICEF, IDS & Anthrologica.

Belief in God should lead us to build health infrastructure to prevent large-scale public health emergencies. John F. Kennedy once said, "Man holds in his mortal hands the power to abolish all forms of human poverty and all forms of human life".[9] It is in our power as physicians and public health specialists to build health systems in order to ensure the health and wellbeing of populations. This is in line with Matthew 25, where Christ commands us to visit prisoners, heal the sick, feed the hungry, and so on. Unless there is significant investment in health systems, we are unable to obey Christ.

I have struggled with the tension between focusing on individuals who require specialized services in resource-poor settings, versus focusing on the needs of the population. In 2011, I heard the story of a young boy named Adam from the Democratic Republic of the Congo. He developed a large facial tumour, which obscured most of his features. He was mocked by his peers, ridiculed and ostracized. A nurse who helped care for him shared his story with my younger sister, who was in her Sunday school class. My sister, who was a teenager at the time, called me and told me, "Surely, there is something we can do to help this young boy!" I immediately contacted my friend Dr Abigail Estelle, who runs a charity called Willing and Abel. This charity does incredible work, providing surgical services to children in developing nations, linking them with specialist centres, and assisting with visas, passports, transportation, and finances. Abi quickly mobilized resources that enabled Adam to fly to Sierra Leone, where an Ear, Nose, and Throat (ENT) surgeon would evaluate whether he could resect the disfiguring tumour that plagued him. Many people contributed financially to ensure that Adam and his grandmother would be able to travel to Sierra Leone, and they closely followed his case. One morning, I received an email from Abi, that included a letter from the surgeon:

---

[9] Inaugural Address of John F. Kennedy, 20 January 1961.

Adam presented to us in Sierra Leone on the M/V Africa Mercy (Mercy Ships) on 15 September 2011 with the history of a tumour growth on the left side of his neck since early 2009. As we understood from the history, he has had two operations to this area before and three courses of chemotherapy. He first came to my attention on 27 July 2011 through the charity Willing and Abel. We agreed to examine and assess him for possible surgery if there was still no evidence of metastases of the tumour which we understood he did not have at that stage. Soon after arrival on the ship a contrast CT was done of the neck, as well as the spine and brain and he was assessed clinically. The surgeons involved in his care discussed the possible surgical treatment at length and came to the conclusion that his clinical condition was beyond a curative procedure and even a palliative procedure; the tumour had invaded almost the entire left side of the neck, enveloping all the vital structures including the common and internal carotid arteries and the internal jugular vein. The tumour had infiltrated the area around the internal carotid artery, that would have made the control and prevention of a fatal hemorrhage almost impossible. We will make him as comfortable as possible and arrange for his travel home to his country.

I was devastated by this news and could only imagine how a young eight-year-old boy felt about having to prepare for death, when all he wanted was to lead a normal life. He wanted a normal childhood, one where he could run, play, and attend school just like any other little boy. He wanted his grandmother Rosalie (who didn't know he could hear her) to stop crying at night.

The staff on Mercy Ships cried as he got off the boat and headed back to Kinshasa. Unfortunately, Ethiopian Airlines would not let him get on the plane as he "smelled" (the odour coming from his infected tumour). How could anyone treat a child like this?

Adam passed away on 8 December. His grandmother tells the following story. The night before his death, he woke up the whole household to pray at 12 midnight. He led everyone in prayer and afterwards he started singing the following song (translated from French): "God is faithful I believe it. By his word, he leads me. God is faithful and I'll put my trust in him". He then went to bed. Around 2 a.m., his grandmother woke up and checked on him. He was gone. I believe sending him to Sierra Leone was the right thing to do, despite the negative outcome. Medicine is an art of probability, as Osler says.

I believe we are to do all that we can to relieve the suffering of those we serve with compassion. Suffering should never be viewed as a curse, rather an opportunity for us to get closer to God and to ultimately become stronger in our faith. It also provides a unique opportunity to bear the burdens of those who need our compassion. Oswald Chamber states, "Never focus your eyes on the obstacle or the difficulty. The obstacle will be a matter of total indifference to the river that will flow steadily through you if you will simply remember to stay focused on the Source".[10] Focusing on "the Source" allows us to be strong when we are weak, and to allow Christ's power to rest in us.

---

[10] Oswald Chambers, *My Utmost for His Highest, the Far-Reaching Rivers of Life* (Lancashire, UK: Discovery House Publishers, 2008), 6 September devotional.

# CHAPTER 5

# DISASTERS, BLAME, AND FORGIVENESS

## (WITH SPECIAL REFERENCE TO THE "LOCKERBIE DISASTER")

### JOHN MOSEY[1]

**M**uch of what I have to say relates directly or indirectly to our family's experiences in a specific disaster. I hope that it will be an apt illustration of much that has been said in this book and that it will provide some useful, first-hand, practical insights.

## Background

I was born in the city of Coventry while the Nazi bombs were raining down. After leaving grammar school, I went into the aircraft industry as a technical illustrator and completed the five-year, day release, City & Guilds course at the Lanchester College of Art and Technology. I often ate my lunchtime sandwiches in the nearby ruins of the old, bombed-out cathedral, which were dominated by the cross of charred beams that had been erected above the smashed altar after the air raid, with the words, "Father Forgive" beneath it. Little did I think then that a day would

---

[1] The author is especially grateful to Dr Davina Miller for her editorial help in this chapter.

come in my life when I would have to give some serious thought to this subject of "forgiveness": what it is and what it is not.

In 1966, I married a German girl called Lisa who had come to Coventry for nursing and midwifery training. She had already had to learn some very serious lessons about forgiveness, and being forgiven, for being a member of a nation that had done so much evil. She was born in Upper Silesia, an eastern part of Germany which became a part of Poland at the end of the war. As a very small child she, along with her mother and three siblings, had been forced to flee westwards to Lower Silesia by the advancing Russian army. After living under Russian military occupation for one year, they were "ethnically cleansed" by the new Polish regime and deported to a blitzed West Germany. Many of the people being deported were slaughtered by the Poles en route. Lisa, her siblings, and her mother were fortunate and grateful.

Lisa and I have two children: Marcus, who was 16 when disaster struck our family, and Helga, who was 19 (see Figure 5.1). Helga was a fine musician. Although expert on the recorder, violin, and piano, her main love was singing. Her lovely mezzo soprano voice was in demand. She sang with one of the country's leading Bach choirs, and was selected from all of the schools in Britain to sing in the National Youth Choir. Her ambition was to sing professionally, and her music professor at Lancaster University said that he had little doubt that she would have made her mark on the music world. She had decided to take a gap year, was working as a nanny with a family in New Jersey in the USA, and had come home for one week before Christmas to collect her school music prize and to meet up with her friends who had already gone up to universities.

## Helga's flight

We had had a wonderful week. I was the taxi driver taking her to various events and friends' homes. I drove her down to Heathrow airport on 21 December to see her off for another few months in the USA where she was going to be singing in a Christmas production with the New Jersey Choral Arts Society. That evening the phone rang and a lady from our church, who had seven sons and loved Helga as the daughter she had always wanted, asked me if Helga had got away all right. I answered, "Yes", and asked, "Why?" She told me that there had been a plane crash in Scotland.

We will never forget that Christmas. The first emotion I remember as I turned on the TV to catch the news at 9 p.m. was one of sympathy for the passengers and crew of the crashed airliner and for the people of the small Scottish town of Lockerbie on which it had fallen, the resulting flames and destruction of which we were viewing (Figure 5.2). Our son, Marcus, sat on the sofa while Lisa perched on the arm. I stood beside her. "How awful, the poor people!" I remember someone saying. Then we began to get details: "Pan Am Flight 103 flying from London to New York, has exploded above the Scottish Borders at about three minutes past seven, raining its debris down on the town of Lockerbie".

"That's Helga's flight", burst from Lisa's lips. Even though I had driven our 19-year-old daughter down to Heathrow airport from our home near Birmingham only a few hours earlier, and had actually checked her luggage in at the Pan Am desk, the possibility of such a thing happening to her just hadn't crossed my mind. These things happen to others; they never happen to you! We are normally observers of other people's tragedies. That is an entirely other world out there on the television; it has nothing to do with us. You can imagine the stunned silence which followed as the unthinkable slowly expanded, filling not only our minds but every nerve and cell of our bodies.

"No! No! No! No!" broke the silence as Marcus screamed at the screen.

"Helga, Helga, Helga". The words quietly managed to escape from somewhere deep down inside my wife. Later, she said that the one time her girl had needed her most, she wasn't there. I stood as if dumb, unable to articulate at all.

The newsflash ended, and the world moved on to other, seemingly trivial matters: how many millions were being spent this Christmas using credit cards, sport, and the weather.

We switched the TV off. I remember saying something about asking God to help us, and the three of us standing together in the middle of the room with our arms around each other as we lifted broken and perplexed hearts to God in prayer. Now, 30 years along the road, we can say with assurance that God has certainly helped us. That life-changing Christmas was the beginning of a journey which we never wanted but which has never ceased to amaze us.

## The aftermath

Within minutes the doorbell and telephone were ringing. Two months earlier, after almost 14 very happy years, we had left our church to help a smaller, struggling church nearby. We were still living in the same house. In the three hours before midnight, over 40 people came to share in our grief. Some stayed just a few silent minutes, some prayed with us and tried to encourage us, others fell apart, and we had to hold them together. This living stream of support continued for several weeks, making us glad that we were part of such a very real spiritual family.

In the weeks that followed, on a daily basis, letters, cards, and faxes poured onto our breakfast table from across the nations. Each morning we would open the 10–20 envelopes which the bewildered postman had delivered. The messages that helped us most seemed to be the ones that made us cry.

I was a gone-to-seed mountaineer and desperately wanted to pack my rucksack and go and look for Helga. We did not know whether her body had been found or if she had been blown to pieces. I decided to let my head rule my heart and stay at home to care for my family and my congregation.

## Christmas 1988

I had prepared my Christmas sermon some days before our daughter's death. As I stood to deliver it on Christmas morning it dawned on me how apt it was. It was entitled "The Empty Chair in

Heaven". I had decided to speak from the Bible verse, "when the fullness of time had come, God sent forth his Son" (Galatians 4:4, ESV). With tears in my eyes, I spoke about how the Father gave up, in a sense, the immediate fellowship of his Son for 33 years. The temporary parting with our daughter and the empty chair in our home gave me some sense of relating, in human terms, to God's situation. The certainty of a reunion with Helga in some form in eternity has always been one of our main supports.

On Christmas Day 1988, we followed our usual routine, but with little appetite and heavy hearts. How we missed Helga's laugh, her musical accompaniment on the recorder, and her lovely voice as we sang around the Christmas tree. Marcus handed out the beautifully wrapped packages: "To dad with love from Helga and Marcus", a pair of gloves, almost too precious to wear; "To mum with love from Helga", a warm winter night dress bought in New York. We sat quietly, desperately holding the last tangible expressions of her love for us.

We will never forget that Christmas: it has become the pivot of our lives. In a smaller but more personal way it is somehow like that first Christmas in world history which made everything become either BC or AD. For us, Christmas 1988 has become the watershed which separates all the events and memories of our lives. Fortunately, feelings change or develop as the distance from the event lengthens, but the echoes of those immediate emotions can still be heard. They are not silenced by the generations of other more logical thoughts, fears, hopes, joys, and aspirations to which they gave birth. We remember the overwhelming assurance that, although we did not understand why God had allowed this to happen, and we certainly didn't like it, somehow he knew all about it and we could trust him.

A few months later, someone said to my wife, "Haven't you got over it yet?" The loss of someone whom you love very much isn't like an illness you "get over". It is more like an amputation which you learn to live with. We will walk with a limp for the rest of our lives, but, with God's help, we might just become better people for it.

I want to address three aspects of dealing with disaster:

- The question of accountability and blame.
- The importance of forgiveness.
- The active, personal response (getting added value out of your disaster).

## Accountability and blame

Naturally, one of the first questions that comes into your head after a disaster is, "Who did this?" The need to have someone to blame is endemic in our human nature. I do not think that there is anything wrong in seeking to apportion blame. Knowing who is responsible is the only way to make sure that steps can be taken to prevent it from happening again, and, on a more personal level, it is the only way in which we can know who we might need to forgive. Punishment doesn't come into the picture here but compensation or solatium, a more meaningful word, might.

Blame can only be attributed if a number of conditions have been met: if (a) the person or persons have either a moral responsibility in the matter or have been appointed to a position of responsibility; (b) they have the ability and means to carry out that responsibility; or (c) the disaster occurs because they failed to carry out their responsibility, either deliberately or through negligence.

In the case of "Lockerbie" there are three parties who, I feel, should share the blame. They are, in reverse order of seriousness: the bombers for doing it; the airline for inadequate security; and the UK and US governments and their agencies set up to protect the public for failing to prevent it, or even deliberately allowing it to happen.

Amazingly, there has been no full and independent inquiry into all relevant matters before and after the event. Prime Minister Margaret Thatcher told us that there would never be an independent inquiry into this disaster. This has resulted in a situation where not all of the three major parties with obvious responsibilities have been thoroughly examined and made answerable for their behaviour.

The perceived perpetrator, Libya, who, after attending the two-year trial and first appeal in Holland – I am 98 per cent convinced was not guilty – has been brought to court, tried, and has paid out considerable compensation to the relatives of the dead and their lawyers as well as being punished through violent sanctions. However, the Scottish Criminal Case Review Commission has given six grounds on which there may have been a serious miscarriage of justice.

The airline, Pan Am, have, to some extent, faced examination and paid for its pathetic security with a payout under the Montreal Convention, and subsequently with its very existence.

The third party with serious responsibility comprises the governments of the USA and the UK and their agencies which had a duty of care toward their citizens. This party has not been thoroughly investigated regarding the execution of its responsibilities in this matter, nor has it been charged with the need to make any reparation at all.

At least 10 warnings were logged by the Federal Aviation Authority and other departments. An anonymous phone call to the US Embassy in Helsinki on 5 December gave accurate details of the bomb, which airline, which route, and a time window of two weeks in which it would be deployed. Paul Channon, the Transport Secretary, even had a photograph of a similar bomb from the German authorities and sent it in the Christmas post to Heathrow security instead of by special courier. It arrived days after the event. The only response to these multiple warnings was to advise some European US Embassy staff not to fly with Pan Am during the Christmas period and to transfer Pik Botha, the South African Foreign Minister, and his entourage who were travelling to the United Nations, to another flight. Nobody warned us. We have been told that Pan Am Flight 103 was the only flight of any airline crossing the Atlantic Ocean in the week before Christmas that had any empty seats. It was only about two-thirds full. My daughter got a ticket at an almost give-away price.

In the Fatal Accident Inquiry relating to the Lockerbie Air Disaster, Sheriff Principal John S. Mowat QC on numerous occasions determined that if certain actions had been in place, these "might have" and "could have" prevented the disaster.[2] If this is true, should not those who had the information and the ability to prevent it, but did absolutely nothing except to warn some important people, be chargeable? If this is true, Lockerbie happened either because the relevant authorities failed to take their responsibilities seriously or because they conspired to deliberately let it happen. In either case, should they not be exposed to some form of serious investigation and be brought to some sort of justice?

Many of the great thinkers of history emphasize the importance of accountability. For example, the French playwright and poet Molière is often quoted as saying, "It is not only what we do, but also what we do not do, for which we are accountable". The eighteenth-century political activist and theorist Thomas Paine averred, "A body of men holding themselves accountable to nobody ought not to be trusted by anybody".[3] The Indian lawyer and political activist Mahatma Gandhi counselled, "It is wrong and immoral to seek to escape the consequences of one's acts".[4] Finally, the American politician Carl Levin is often quoted as asserting that "Restoring responsibility and accountability is essential to the economic and fiscal health of our nation".

For some of us, "Who did it?" has never been the most important question: a far greater crime has been perpetrated. The

---

[2] Sheriffdom of South Strathclyde, Dumfries and Galloway Determination by Sheriff Principal John S. Mowat QC in the Fatal Accident Inquiry Relating to the Lockerbie Air Disaster (1991), pp. 1–47.

[3] Thomas Paine, "Rights of Man: Being an Answer to Mr. Burke's Attack on the French Revolution – part 7", *US History*: https://www.ushistory.org/paine/rights/c1-016.htm (last viewed 11 November 2019).

[4] Mahatma Gandhi, Judith M. Brown (ed.), *The Essential Writings* (Oxford, UK: Oxford University Press, 2008), p. 251.

really big question is "Why was this 'preventable disaster' allowed to happen?" The request for a locus in which this question could be asked, let alone answered, has consistently been refused by our politicians. As mentioned, there has been no traditional, independent inquiry into the largest peacetime mass killing in the UK. Our efforts to get an answer have been reinforced by the information in the Helsinki warning which meant that the authorities knew what to look for, where to look, and when to look – and did nothing. Why was nothing done to either prevent the disaster or to warn the public? We have been forced down the important but subsidiary road of questioning the verdict and attacking the Scottish legal system. We do not seek severe punishment for individuals, but simply some transparency and honesty from those who have, for all of these years, provided only prevarications, obfuscations, and plain lies.

## The importance of forgiveness

It was not until the following evening that we realized that we were going to be a focus for media attention. A TV news team arrived at our home and asked if they could interview us. There were already rumours that a bomb might have been the cause of the disaster, and some of the relatives were howling for blood. We were asked how we felt about it and said that we readily forgave whoever was responsible. "How can you forgive animals like that?" was one interviewer's response. While I was trying to formulate a reply, Lisa said, "Sir, Jesus said in the Sermon on the Mount, 'If you do not forgive men their trespasses, neither will your Father forgive your trespasses.' We haven't murdered anyone, but we are big sinners who are having to trust in the death and resurrection of Jesus Christ as our only hope of forgiveness and heaven. We just dare not fool about with not forgiving".

Then he shot another question at me. "You are a Christian minister. Has this not destroyed your faith?"

"Well", I said, "This is where we prove whether what we have preached for most of our lives is real, or whether it is just a game".

Unforgiveness is a cancer; a killer. It wrecks lives; it wrecks families; it wrecks communities; and it wrecks international relationships.

To forgive someone who has wronged us is not usually an easy thing to do. Forgiveness is usually a process. I was once bullied over a period of time by someone I worked with, and it took me eight years of hard work to reach a place of real forgiveness and restored friendship. In the Lockerbie case it was immediate and total. I would say it was miraculous. One of the greatest aids to forgiving is understanding why we should forgive. Here are just three good reasons. The first one comes from a purely Christian viewpoint but the others are simply common sense.

## We all need forgiveness

It is clear from reading the Bible, and the teachings of Jesus in particular, that forgiveness and reconciliation are a huge part of God's agenda. The Sermon on the Mount is acclaimed widely, even by those of other or no religious persuasions, as being one of the very finest codes for living. Jesus was so serious about this that, directly after giving us the Lord's Prayer, he gave it double emphasis and made it a condition of God's forgiveness: "For if you forgive others their trespasses, your heavenly Father will also forgive you, but if you do not forgive others their trespasses, neither will your Father forgive your trespasses" (Matthew 6:14–15, ESV). For Christians, lack of forgiveness is never an option. We have a debt to pay: "and be kind to one another, tenderhearted, forgiving one another, just as God in Christ has forgiven you" (Ephesians 4:32, ESV).

George Herbert, the seventeenth-century poet and theologian, put it so well: "He who cannot forgive breaks the bridge over which he himself must walk".[5]

---

[5] Sidney Lee (ed.), *The Autobiography of Edward, Lord Herbert of Cherbury*, revised edition (London: Routledge, 1906), p. 34.

## Forgiveness sets people free

Have you ever carried a burden of guilt and then felt the huge relief of being told that you are forgiven? One of my earliest memories of personal emotion was from being five or six years old when food was still rationed after the war. I crept down the stairs in the middle of the night, took the packet of Rowntree's jelly from the cupboard, carefully broke off one segment and put it in my mouth. It was delicious. I returned the remainder to the packet and put it back on the shelf. The following Sunday, friends were coming for tea, so mum took out the jelly. "John, have you been at this jelly?" Horror struck me. "No, mum. It must have been Roger". Roger was my two-year-old brother! I still remember the feelings that followed. For several days I couldn't look my mother in the face. I had lied to her, and I suppose that I was ashamed. The Sun stopped shining and the birds stopped singing. It was a painful time. Some days later, my mother said to me, "John, I know that it was you who took the jelly but I still love you and you are forgiven". It had been a lime jelly and the juice had run from my mouth and down my pillow, leaving a green stain. "Beware your sin will find you out!"

Someone once said that the power to forgive is the prerogative of gods and kings. It is certainly a very great tool in the effort to bring about peace and happiness in our world. This could hardly have been better expressed than by William Shakespeare in his play, *The Merchant of Venice*. In Act 4, Scene 1 he puts these words into the mouth of Portia as she pleads for Antonio. Mercy is a close relative to forgiveness.

> The quality of mercy is not strained,
> It droppeth as the gentle rain from heaven
> Upon the place beneath. It is twice blest:
> It blesseth him that gives, and him that takes.
> 'Tis mightiest in the mightiest, it becomes
> The thronéd monarch better than his crown.
> His sceptre shows the force of temporal power,

The attribute to awe and majesty,
Wherein doth sit the dread and fear of kings;
But mercy is above this sceptred sway.
It is enthronéd in the hearts of kings,
It is an attribute to God Himself,
And earthly power doth then show likest God's
When mercy seasons justice. Therefore, Jew,
Though justice be thy plea, consider this:
That in the course of justice, none of us
Should see salvation. We do pray for mercy,
And that same prayer doth teach us all to render
The deeds of mercy.

Forgiveness is a double blessing. It blesses both giver and recipient. Indeed, the one who gives often receives the greater blessing. As the Bible says, "It is more blessed to give than to receive" (Acts 20:35).

After 27 years in Robben Island prison, Nelson Mandela said, "As I walked out the door toward the gate that would lead to my freedom, I knew if I didn't leave my bitterness and hatred behind, I'd still be in prison".[6] Lack of forgiveness causes bitterness which destroys our peace. It is like a secondary infection which can cause more damage than the offence which we refuse to forgive.

When I was young, one of my friends had to have his appendix removed. The operation was successful, but a few days later he had to return to the hospital because of secondary infections. A week later he died, not from the original appendicitis but from the secondary infection. As a minister and sometime trauma counsellor, I have seen people's lives destroyed, not by the bad things that have happened to them but by the anger

---

[6] Kweku Mandela, "My grandfather taught me forgiveness", *HuffPost*: https://www.huffpost.com/entry/my-grandfather-taught-me-_b_4994928 (last viewed 6 November 2019).

and bitterness that they fostered and would not let go. The only person we hurt by harbouring anger and resentment is oneself. The perpetrator of the offence either does not know how we feel or, if they do know, they do not care. They might even be glad. I would encourage anyone to let it go; don't pay them interest on their investment in hurting us.

The following extract is from a wonderful article written by journalist Ron Ferguson, which was published in the Scottish newspaper, *The Herald*, on 18 November 2003:

"The grace to do the impossible".

IMAGINE that you have a 19-year-old daughter. She is the pride and joy of your life, more precious to you than life itself, even. You have watched her move from babyhood to the toddler stage, through primary and secondary school, and on to university. You have seen her flourish as her natural talents have developed. Now she is on the cusp of open possibilities. Her future is very much part of your future.

… You're sitting at home watching television. A newsflash causes your heartbeat to accelerate. An aircraft has gone down. Can it be the one that she is on? You make frantic telephone calls, but the lines are jammed. The news reports say that all of the passengers are believed dead. Please, God, let it not be her plane. But it is: she is dead; not only that, murdered. A bomb… Could you ever find it in your heart to forgive the bastard who did this foul deed?…

This is not something that most of us, thankfully, will have to face. The Rev'd. John Mosey's 19-year-old daughter, Helga, was one of the 270 people killed in the bombing of Pan Am Flight 103 over Lockerbie on that unforgettable night…. "We are all sinners who need forgiveness", he said. "Americans use the word 'closure', but that's not a word I'm comfortable with. The rawness of our loss has gone, but we have suffered an amputation, and we have learned to walk with a limp, a limp we will walk with for the rest of our lives".

For John Mosey, being a clergyman would not have made life easier. In fact, there would be more pressure on him, because Christians are "supposed" to forgive even their worst enemies. People would be watching this man to see if he was living up to the fearsome demands of his faith; while through the night he would be repeatedly picturing a fanatic getting a bomb onto that aircraft and blowing his dear one to smithereens…. The fact that her death was one among 270 would have been no consolation. I'm not sure that I could pass that test. I have never understood those who say that Christianity is an easy religion, and that people sign up to it because it offers cheap consolation. "Ye have heard that it hath been said, Thou shall love thy neighbour, and hate thine enemy. But I say unto you, love your enemies, bless them that curse you, do good to them that hate you, and pray for them which despitefully use you; that ye may be children of your father which is in heaven". Easy? Really?

… Yet that same impossible command gets right under the skin. We have seen the effects of entrenched hatred in Northern Ireland; there is no doubt that the situation there has been partially redeemed by the forgiveness exercised by people such as Gordon Wilson, whose daughter was a victim of the Enniskillen atrocity. And the spiral of tit-for-tat violence in the Middle East can only be broken by forgiveness, as well as justice.

… Hannah Arendt's distinction between the need to forgive the person who has wounded us, while continuing to condemn what the person has done, needs to be kept in mind… yet forgiveness of offenders by their victims can often have the most creative and redeeming effects.

Nelson Mandela's pardon of his captors has had enormous redemptive consequences. Speaking of a visit to Robben Island, Richard Holloway said that he was choked by the enormity of Mandela's graciousness. "Those are the conditions that normally produce enraged avengers, whose actions we deplore, yet whose embittered logic we can understand. The enormity of forgiveness flowing from such conditions is impossible to understand. It is the insanity of grace".

This is a frail flowering when set against the powerfully entrenched hatreds of our day, linked as they are with the portable technology of mass slaughter. When we witness the impossible possibility of the forgiveness of sworn enemies we know we are in the presence of awesome, sacred, business. The insanity of grace is the only sanity available to us now.

During the Lockerbie trial I spoke frequently in my very limited and faltering Arabic with the family of one of the men charged with the bombing, Mr Abdelbaset Al Megrahi. Whatever his guilt or otherwise, they were going through a very difficult time. While he was in prison in Scotland I wrote to him on a number of occasions and, through the good offices of the Libyan Chargé d'affaires in Glasgow we had two telephone conversations. I told him that I didn't think he was guilty but that even if he was – and only he and God (and perhaps one other) knew the truth – as far as my family was concerned, he was forgiven. He wanted me to visit him but the authorities, quite illegally, would not allow it.

## Forgiveness and the law

Forgiveness is a personal thing but the law must not forgive. It must pursue, prosecute, and punish the wrongdoer. The Bible clearly teaches that the civic law is God's protection for society, and that those who administer it are his servants. Even to the Christians in the wicked Rome of Nero, Paul wrote, "those authorities that exist have been instituted by God. Therefore whoever resists authority resists what God has appointed… It is the servant of God to execute wrath on the wrongdoer" (Romans 13:1–2, 4). Beat me up and steal my wallet and I will forgive you, but I can't stop the police officer from taking you away to prison.

Although their methods may sometimes be open to question, governments are right in seeking to bring to justice the instigators of horrendous crimes and those who aid and abet them, but the moment the desire for revenge obscures this aim, they become little better than the terrorists and will only promote the cycle of violence. The ultimate justice we leave to a higher court before which we all must, one day, stand.

As we saw earlier, we are encouraged to forgive as God forgives: that is, with grace; free and undeserved favour. Forgiveness does not demand repentance, but it does the offender little good if it is not accepted and its need acknowledged. God has thrown a lifebelt into the ocean of this world's sin and depravity, but it does no good to the person who refuses to accept and make use of it.

## The active, personal response

Sitting at Helga's desk in her room very early on the fifth morning after the disaster, I found myself mulling over the previous night's cries for revenge as the news came out that it was a bomb that had brought down the plane. "Nuke the Arabs". Some wanted the Middle East blasted off the planet.

"I don't want to be like that", I thought. "If I want someone dead because my daughter is dead I reduce myself to the level of the terrorists; I make myself no better than they are". Some words, purportedly and often quoted as those of Mahatma Gandhi, came to mind: "An eye for an eye and the world will soon be blind".[7]

---

[7] Fred Shapiro (ed.), *The Yale Book of Quotations* (New Haven, CT: Yale University Press, 2006), p. 270, footnote 1.

"But I have to do something". Looking back, I suppose that I was really trying to find a strategy on which to base my survival of this awful blow.

Some weeks before I had been reading *Markings*, the journals of Dag Hammarskjöld, the Secretary-General of the United Nations from 1953–1961, and suddenly something that he had written came forcibly back to me. "The question is not: why did it happen this way, or where is it going to lead you, or what is the price you will have to pay. It is simply: how are you making use of it".[8] I don't remember how, but I found myself reading Paul's letter to the Romans, chapter 12, verse 21, "Do not be overcome by evil, but overcome evil with good", and I thought, "That's how I win!" A few days later, I wrote the following article for the local newspaper based on those thoughts. The film *The Empire Strikes Back* was doing the rounds for the second time.

### THE KINGDOM STRIKES BACK

John F. Mosey, 8 January 1989

Flight 103; Lockerbie. Nothing can alter the dreadful facts. But now, to the grief and bewilderment is added the cry for revenge. On last evening's news we heard: "Nuke the Arabs, blast the Middle East off the planet… etc". Certainly, the guilty parties must be brought to justice. Others of similar mind must be deterred. However, we do not seek a personal revenge against those who have so roughly snatched our nineteen year old daughter from us. If we take personal revenge against our human enemies we reduce ourselves to their level and merely add evil to evil. No, our anger must be directed, not against the small-fry who plant bombs,

---

[8] Dag Hammarskjöld, *Markings* (London: Faber and Faber, 1964), p. 135.

but against the Arch-Terrorist, the enemy, of mankind, the spiritual force behind all the world's evils, who the Bible calls "Satan". But how can we strike back against such a one? Threats do not alarm him, bullets cannot hurt him; but when we try to live according to the principles of God's Kingdom, he shakes with fear. The most effective way of striking back is clearly stated in the last verse of the twelfth chapter of Paul's letter to the Christians at Rome who were having a pretty torrid time under the emperor Nero. He says, "Don't be overcome by evil, overcome evil by doing good". This is the only way to cancel out evil.

I believe that, by right reactions, the good that can come will far outweigh the mountain of evil and suffering that so many are experiencing today.

I had recently been appointed to our denomination's Overseas Missions Board as co-director for missions and humanitarian relief in Asia, and was becoming increasingly aware of the enormous needs in that part of the world and was doing my best to motivate people to support a number of projects.

In the weeks following Christmas, the Helga Mosey Memorial Trust for the care and education of needy children was set up. Kind cheques from friends, churches, schools, and local businesses began to pour through our letterbox. It is now a registered charity. A beautiful home in the Philippines was built for abandoned and abused children. The Philippine Social Services have said that if our daughter was still alive, more than half of the 200-plus children who have passed through the home in the past 25 years would be dead. When my wife and I visit there and see those healthy and loved children, we have something back and feel that the enemy has been robbed. On a recent visit I met some of the children from the home who were now in their twenties and had trained in various employments. One girl, now 24, who had been horribly sexually abused was a qualified social worker, married with two children. A similar home has been set up in India and investments have been made in health and educational projects in a number of countries blighted by poverty or war.

What better way of striking back at evil can there be than to bless some of its saddest victims? Don't be overcome by evil, overcome evil by doing good. [9]

---

[9] For further reading: an especially fine article has been written on the subject of blame and responsibility by Dr Garrath Williams, lecturer in Ethics at Lancaster University, in Vol. 3, M-R of the Encyclopedia of Applied Ethics. Those interested in the "Lockerbie" question should read the excellent paper by Dr Davina Miller (2011) "Who knows about this? Western policy towards Iran: The Lockerbie case", Defense and Security Analysis, December, Vol. 27, Iss. 4; and John Ashton, *Megrahi: You Are My Jury* (Edinburgh, UK: Birlinn, 2012); and Prof. Robert Black QC's weekly BLOG, rblackqc@gmail.com.

# CHAPTER 6

# HAITIAN WOMANHOOD, FAITH, AND EARTHQUAKES

## MARIE AND LUCIE

To record Haitian culture and society as patriarchal portrays an unreality on the ground. Women are the *potomitan* of society, a term that is rooted in the historic status of Haitian Vodou spirituality but which, in sociological-speak, also means that women are the centre-post of society, just like the *potomitan* is the centre-post of the *peristil* (Vodou temple). Expected to remain monogamous, unlike the men, women also have responsibility for income generation and for the productivity of the home. Hence, many Haitian women run small, informal sector businesses either from their homes or by becoming street vendors (*marchanns*). Those women who manage to navigate through the educational systems of their country (a minority of women, it must be said), mostly run by private, faith-based schools, can find employment in the extensive garment industries. These industries are often outsourced by manufacturers in the USA with an eye for cheap labour. They offer remuneration that is low but better than being unemployed. Some women will succeed in gaining employment in the healthcare, education, financial, and even in the political sectors if they succeed in their higher education, or in upward mobility through "who they know" more than "what they know".

With perhaps the notable exception of the last category just mentioned, life for women in Haiti is extremely tough. They are often the subjects of gender-based violence, mainly from men with whom they are in relationships. Many men, for their part, believe that they are legitimately able to subject their partners to physical "discipline". They believe that women should just accept this as being normal life under Haitian culture. Therefore, generally life for women has been tough, but for us personally not so much from men as it has been for many other women.

## About us

Our names are Marie and Lucie (see Figure 6.1).[1] We are mother and daughter, and we have lived in the capital city of Haiti, Port-au-Prince, pretty well all of our life so far. We were there when the terrible earthquake shook our city and our whole nation, back on 12 January 2010, a date that is indelibly imprinted into our psyches. You know how it is: we all have a single experience that we know exactly where we were when it happened, the day and even the time it happened. If the trauma of what happened has not succeeded in erasing our memories to protect us, we even remember in detail what happened. This is how it seems for both of us. We would like to share with you our story around that date, day, and time of the Haiti earthquake of 2010.

It is important for you to know that we did not know what an earthquake was before that dreadful day. Now, for sure, we do know! We might not know the science, so to speak: we were never taught that by our education system here, not by our government nor by Catholic or Protestant schools. Whether that is because the last serious earthquake to occur here was over 200 years ago, and/or because we get blown out and soaked out pretty much every year by tropical storms and hurricanes, we are not sure. But it is what it is, as we say. Just do not let what we have just said lead you to think that we ordinary Haitians are idiots. What we do not know is mainly due to what we have not been told. Often with our political system here, important information is

---

[1] The authors have confirmed their wish to use their real names.

given out only on "a need to know" basis – and too often we, the general public, and us being women as well, are deemed to be those who do not need to know.

Now let us tell you our stories, as survivors of one of the most devastating earthquakes, from a human loss perspective, in modern times. We will take it in turns, at various points, to share, and at times we shall speak as one.

## Upbringing

I, Marie, was born and brought up here in Port-au-Prince. I am the firstborn of eight kids: seven brothers and one sister. My parents were Christians, so you could say I was also brought up in our church, a Baptist church. In my twenties, I became a regular member of the church choir, which sang at each Sunday service, and I also took part in church choir competitions. I love to sing of and for Jesus! At the time, there was no prospect for advancing above primary school so I did not have a secondary education. Even so, somehow, I was able to get to study medical field auxiliary science, and that landed me with a good job... until the earthquake, that is.

I married a man with whom I also went on to have two children, both girls. Lucie is the youngest, she was 15 years old when the earthquake struck; at the time, her sister was 24 and she had a baby boy. My husband, just eight months after Lucie was born, left us for another woman. He even divorced me without me knowing! In 2004, he disappeared without trace. It was at the time a coup d'état ousted Jean-Bertrand Aristide, our then-president, a very dangerous period in our history.

Since their father left me when they were very young, I have had to raise my daughters on my own, with the help of my sister, their aunt. We four are the principal actors in this story, as well as God, of course.

Now I, Lucie, am so happy to be able to join my mum in sharing our stories, even though it involves recalling the most awful moments of my life. Since my father left our home very early on, I have not known what it is to have a father. I am very close to my mum and love her so much. I also love my sister and especially the child she bore in 2009, to make me an aunt. At the time, that was one of the highlights of my life. Life for us as a family was very happy, even though it was often far from easy. I can recall, around when I was 13 years old, a hurricane came through our area. Our house at that time had just a tin-sheet roof. The winds blew away the tin-sheets, and so our house and all our belongings got soaked in the torrential rain that hurricanes bring. We had to move in with a friend of my mum, into her house. For some reason that is when I began to feel unwell. I was not happy. I started to have bad dreams. I experienced other difficulties in my life too, until we rented a house and went to live there. That same year I became an aunt to my sister's new baby boy. I cannot describe to you how happy that made me! I doted upon him! What is more, this was a time of transformation for me. It was when I began to hold firm to my Christian faith.

## The earthquake

Neither of us was at home at the time of the earthquake. It was Tuesday, 12 January 2010. I, Marie, was travelling around the city with my work. I had gone to measure the blood pressure of two of my clients. When I had done that, at around 4 p.m., I had gone to take my usual place, under the gallery of a building in town, where I would sit to conduct my small business as a *machann*. We set up our stalls there, by the side of the busy street, but in the shade of the gallery to protect us from the sun. For some reason – let us call it intuition – I felt that I should return to my home. To do this I needed to take public transportation, which in Haiti is, more often than not, by *tap tap* – a sort of decorated pickup truck with the rear part enclosed and with benches running along each side for passengers to sit on. At the first place I walked to there were no *tap taps* available, so I walked to a second place and, again, no vehicles there either. Walking on to the third location, I managed to find a *tap tap* to take me. Often these vehicles are very crowded, not just with people, but with goods and baggage as well.

When we had reached the football stadium, the vehicle began to shake. In fact, it shook violently, throwing passengers around. At first, I thought another car had hit us, as the force seemed to come from outside the vehicle, not inside. Everyone in the *tap tap* was crying out to "Jesus". After about half a minute, the vehicle stopped and soon the shaking stopped as well. We all got out of the truck. I was lifting up my hands into the air and worshipping Christ, saying, "Thank you, Jesus!" I still thought it had been due to a traffic accident. I had no idea it had been an earthquake, until, that is, I was soon witnessing terrible things going on around me. Buildings were falling down, with concrete block walls and concrete slabbed ceilings collapsing onto people. I saw people with limbs missing, little babies all covered in blood. I even questioned myself, "Is this civil war, or a coup d'état". You might think that strange, but if you know anything about Haitian history, you would know we have had many civil wars and coups! However, I really had no idea about what was happening.

I left the stadium area on foot, to head for our home in Carrefour, a major suburb of the capital, about 6 miles (10 km) away from where I was. It was the first time that I had ever made the journey on foot. I was so used to the *tap tap* driver doing the work that it was not so easy for me to navigate my way on my own. The journey got more upsetting by the fact that as I was walking I witnessed more terror. I saw people jumping out of a bank's second floor windows into the street out of sheer panic over the violent tremors. Then, to add to my discomfort and fear, I suddenly thought about my youngest daughter, Lucie. She was only 15 years old at that time, and she was still at school, so I thought. As I walked, I saw a group of students coming out of a school that had collapsed; many of the students were bathed in blood. This made me even more worried over Lucie, and it made me pray so hard that God would care for my daughter. Therefore, I headed toward her school, but then I remembered that she always walked home from school with a friend. I headed to where this friend lived. In fact, as I got to her street I met the friend. Unfortunately, her mother was stuck beneath the rubble of their house with a broken arm. She told me that Lucie was not with her. Rather she had chosen to continue walking toward her own home, and she pointed me in the direction Lucie had gone. But now I'll let Lucie begin her story of the earthquake.

I, Lucie, was doing well in school, right up until the earthquake happened. In fact, as my mum has said, I was at school that afternoon of the earthquake. My other sister was also in school somewhere else. In Haiti, there are two sessions for students to attend school, one in the morning, the other in the afternoon. That day I was in school for the afternoon session. However, what my mum did not know at the time was that our class attendant had said that we could go home early because the teacher was not coming. Therefore, when the ground began shaking, my friend and I were outside of the school property. The sound of the earthquake made me think that there was a helicopter, or an aeroplane, which had crashed. As previously mentioned, I had no idea what an earthquake was.

My friend and I were in shock as we walked away from the school together, leaving behind, I later found out, a scene in which many of my fellow students had been killed. Furthermore, as we walked along we came across another school and were tempted to go inside it. I thank God that we decided not to, because shortly after we moved on that school collapsed too. I later heard that many students had died in that school collapse.

We soon met my friend's brother, and my friend and her brother both left me as they headed off toward their home. I walked on, in a daze of shock, but praying to God. I wanted to throw off my backpack, to lighten the load I was carrying, which seemed to get much heavier under the trauma I was experiencing and the distance I had to walk to my home. I decided not to do away with the extra load, however, and carried on walking and thinking, "Could this be the end of the world? Is it the ground that is shattering, could the Earth be at an end?" All I could pray was that God would protect me and my mother. I can remember that walk and how all along it there seemed to be nothing left in me, no strength, no emotion. It was as if I had died emotionally.

Thanks to God, my mum did eventually meet up with me on the journey. As we walked together toward our home, we saw buildings that had collapsed: it was horrible! Yet still we did not know what was happening. By this time, I had lost all strength and desire to return to my home. However, my mother felt that she had to return, to see what had happened to my sister and my nephew, to my aunt, and to our house. Around this time, my mum and I came across some friends of hers. It was not until then that we heard these people speaking about it being an earthquake.

## Marie's grandson

We had not been with the friends for very long before my mum suddenly panicked. Her thoughts had gone to her other daughter's whereabouts, as she had also been at a school. My mum was concerned for her grandson, and how the family home had fared in the earthquake. By this time, of course, it was dark, which comes early in the evening in Haiti. Nevertheless, my mum suddenly took off in search of her daughter and the baby. After she had gone, I continued to walk with our friends, knowing now that what had happened was an earthquake. At one point, I could see a foot, caught in the rubble of a collapsed building, just dangling in the air. Would these nightmarish sights never stop? Eventually, we came to a church, but we dared not go inside the building, not straight after an earthquake! Instead, we gathered with other survivors in the open grounds of the church, where we would be safe from falling buildings. But I must let my mum continue her part of this story now.

After leaving Lucie, I was in a terrible state of mind, so worried for my other daughter and her child. When I eventually approached my house – there were three houses side by side – the house to our right, my sister's home, looking from the front, had crumbled down and destroyed our house in the process, trapping my sister and my daughter's baby inside. It was an awful sight.

My sister later told me that when the earthquake shook she had been on the gallery of my house. The building collapsed all around her. After losing and regaining consciousness she became totally disorientated. All she could do was pray that God would protect her and provide a solution. As her coordination returned, she found herself trapped under a plastic chair with the ceiling resting on the top of the chair. She called out for help and a man passing by heard her cries. He turned back and dug a hole in the debris that she was able to crawl out through.

When I saw the state of my house I despaired. I was able to ask another passer-by if he would be willing to go inside the ruins of my house to help find my daughter's baby. He refused to go inside, saying that it would be very dangerous given the current state of the collapsed building. I found this hard to accept, even though it was probably a wise decision for the man to make at that time. I felt so helpless, not being able to do anything to save my grandson, or even if he had died, to retrieve his body. I later came to know that some children lay for days beneath the rubble before being rescued alive and well. I prayed so much that this would be the case with my grandson. Alive or dead, I prayed that God would preserve his body.

My anxiety was not helped by aftershocks recurring throughout the night, with a particularly strong one occurring around midnight. Each aftershock made me pray even more that God would protect my grandson. Yet at the same time as the night wore on, I began to doubt that my grandson would be alive. It was also during the night that I learned from friends that Lucie was safe with friends, and I learned where she was staying, which was some relief for me at least. Let Lucie tell you how the night had passed for her.

For me (Lucie), the night had been very lonely. There were so many tremors, and each time they occurred everybody held onto their loved ones, but I did not have anyone to hold onto. So I held onto myself, and I looked into the sky and prayed.

At one point, I had come across a little boy who had injured his leg, so I prayed for him as well. It was at this location that my other sister managed to locate us sometime during that night. She was in a terrible state. She wanted to know what had happened to her baby, and I and my mum had the awful job of breaking the terrible news to her that we were certain her baby had not survived when the house had collapsed. We were all heartbroken.

## After the earthquake

We all found being together again was a great comfort, but the living conditions became increasingly hard. We tried to make some kind of shelter out of plastic covers supported by sticks of wood. We would alternate between being too hot from the Sun and being soaked by rain. During this period, we found food, mainly from the United Nations (MINUSTAH) teams. I, Marie, managed to get a food card. I had to go to a distribution centre, next to the White House (the president's official house) in the centre of the city. Somehow, I managed to carry a very large bag of rice from that place. Also, my daughter had a friend in the city whose father was a priest. He would come by every two days, carrying a backpack full of food, such as rice and milk.

By February, however, life in Port-au-Prince had become unbearable. There was so much destruction, and so much smell! The stench of so many dead bodies, decaying in the heat of the Sun, hung over the city. Remaining in the city with that smell would have driven us all crazy. Therefore, we made a decision to move to the city of Jacmel, which is about 60 miles (100 km) from the capital, down on the south coast. We went there, dressed only in the clothes we had been wearing since the earthquake, to distract ourselves from the horrors of Port-au-Prince. Mercifully, while we were there my (Marie) brother came from the States, bringing us clothes to wear. Of course, there were no schools functioning – so many schools had been destroyed; so many children and teachers killed and injured.

When we returned to Port-au-Prince, it was April 2010 – three months after the earthquake. We returned to an Internally Displaced Persons (IDP) camp in the Delmas 13 district, to start life all over again in a tent (see Figure 6.2). I (Marie) even managed to get work, continuing my previous job, but not for long. There came a time when the church I was attending was sending a team on a mission trip. I was owed some vacation and I decided to take it. However, not wanting to risk losing my job in my absence, I asked a friend of mine to take my place while I was away. When I came back, I was told to wait, in case there was a possibility for me being called to work. Needless to say, that call never came.

Life in the camp was such a struggle for us. Emotionally, it is hard for us to describe that period. Only by May 2013 were we happy. This is because then we received news that we could move into a rented house, after three terrible years of suffering and waiting.

Living in the IDP camp was very frightening. Situated where we were, very near to the road, we would often hear cars passing, and people passing by who were shouting about there being thieves around. We would pray at night that God would help us to sleep. Thankfully, we did not experience any violence against ourselves during this time. However, we did receive criticism from people because we were living in a tent. People would verbally abuse us because we would not move to the IDP camp set up in front of the White House. There, people felt they would get a higher profile, be an embarrassment to the government, and be more likely to be rehoused sooner. However, we did not want to move. The Delmas site seemed quieter and better for us, even if it meant having to wait for a longer time to be rehoused. It posed a more secure location, less risky, for us. We were sure that God would take care of us there. We remember praying that, despite all the criticism and hardship of life in the Delmas camp, God would lift up our heads, lift up our dignity, and that one day those people who were throwing abuse at us would come to see that God took care of us.

Do not get us wrong, we only felt secure in the camp because we believed God was with us. In many other respects, life was very hard. In the area where we were, we had to take showers behind makeshift screens, and going to the latrines at night was a terrible nightmare for women. Many women and children got abused and raped making that trip. Hygienically, the situation was awful. We felt deprived of our dignity. For me (Marie), it was hard to have my daughter, Lucie, complain, saying, "Mum, I am too young to be living here with those kinds of things going on". I would say in return, "What about me?!" And Lucie would answer, "You too! You are too old!" However, we both knew the situation we were in and we supported each other through it. As women, we knew we were both vulnerable. For example, on one occasion a neighbour in the camp came to us. He had noticed that, in the absence of any privacy in such living conditions, he had seen that we often had no food and did not go around begging. Even when we did cook, he noticed that we cooked inside the hot tent. So he offered us his services: that whenever we wanted food, Lucie should come around and ask. We thanked him and said, "No thanks". With one of us women just a teenager, and a girl, we had offers from men who said that she could stay in their houses. We always turned down such offers. We refused to trade in our dignity and our purity for promises of a comfier life.

Our vulnerability also came from losing friends after the earthquake. This increased our sense of loneliness. Lucie found it hard sustaining relationships during this period. Once people learned where she was living, they would not want to continue friendship with her because living in only a tent brought down the stigma of poverty upon her. The loneliness grew also from friends moving away from the city. We prayed that God would lift up our heads.

I (Lucie) found it hard, socially, living in the IDP camp, separated from my friends a lot of the time. Whenever they asked if they could come to my home, to study with me there, I would tell them it was not possible. I would make an excuse, that I had an uncle and he is strict and would not allow people to visit me there.

The weather could also be threatening. The first time, we were not at home when the winds battered our tent and it fell down. On that occasion, some neighbours cleared up the mess and mended the tent before we returned. Another time there was such heavy rain and strong winds that the tent again risked falling down. We prayed, "Do not allow us to be embarrassed by being left out in the rain".

Through all of this struggle, God has brought us to a time (2013) when we entered a real house – albeit rented. We now have firm walls and ceilings, and we are happy.

## After-effects of the earthquake

It would be good to finish with some reflections on how we have coped psychologically and spiritually through this awful period of our lives. Again, we shall speak separately to give you our experiences.

I, Marie, found I was affected psychologically in part, by my background. The man I married, at the time he left me, had wanted to take Lucie with him. I told him he could not do that, as I wanted her to stay with me. I am so glad of this in view of our experience of the earthquake, and also in view of what I now suspect he may have been into at that time and then his mysterious death back in 2004. I was also affected by the fact I lost my job and all my material possessions when our house collapsed. Furthermore, I did not receive any help from the church. Even though I was in a prayer group since 1980, through all our experience of the earthquake no one from my church ever asked me how I was living with my two daughters. No one came to see the conditions we were living in. But neither did I want to speak to people about it. Only six months prior to leaving the IDP camp did I mention to our pastor the conditions we were living in, and about our bid to find a house and some financial means to live again. In those six months after telling him, we found enough money and we moved out of the camp.

I have always been able to address these problems with prayer. Prayer has been the greatest help to us both. Through all that we went through, and especially in this world, where you need money for everything, I kept on praying and asking God to provide for us. In 2013, after I had lost my job, our home, and our belongings, I prayed and asked God, "How long are you going to allow us to stay living under this tent, because this next year's going to make us four years?" And so, when we were able to move out soon after it was such a joy! I have even met people who have asked me how I do it, how I manage to hold it all together. Even though sometimes I have felt abandoned by God, I respond to those times with prayer. Some of my friends nicknamed me, "Safe Body in Christ", because I was always praying and I stayed with Christ. I will let Lucie speak of her experience now.

There were times when I, Lucie, would feel that God had abandoned me. I did have times when I questioned God's goodness and whether God knew what he was doing, putting us through all of that awful experience. It hurt me especially hard when my little nephew died. We did not find him from under the rubble until nine days after the earthquake struck. His cot was still intact, but he had been knocked out of his cot by the strong vibrations and some blocks had fallen on him. Hearing that hurt me deeply. I had been so pleased to learn I had become an aunt. To make my grief even more painful, when the body of my nephew was removed from the rubble of our house, he was immediately taken to the mass grave at Titanyen. We were all so terribly devastated by everything that had happened in such a short space of time that we did not have the emotional energy to cope with this huge loss or with funeral arrangements. You might find such an admission strange, particularly if you have little experience of life in our country when an earthquake strikes. With so many dead bodies, the capacity of our authorities to cope with such amounts of death was overwhelmed very soon into the first day after the earthquake. The morgue at the General

Hospital in Port-au-Prince was completely overcrowded and so too were the many small, private funeral homes. With the electricity infrastructure now damaged, there was no power for refrigeration in the morgues. People were setting fire to dead bodies that were piling up in the streets. They were afraid that there would be a spread of disease soon if they were left to rot in the hot sunshine. Animals were also beginning to eat bodies. Therefore, our government ordered their lorry driver fleet to load bodies into their trucks and to transport them to the national mass grave at Titanyen, to the north of the city. Our baby was one such body disposed of in this way.

Given how much I loved my nephew, and how much I was looking forward to seeing him grow up to know me as his aunt, I have to say that I did struggle with God at this time. Therefore, yes, there was a period after the earthquake when I used to go with my mum to church, not out of personal conviction, but just to sit and fill an empty spot. I was in a very low place. Then one Sunday my emotions tore at me and I realized that I needed to come to church to get myself into a better place before God. I listened hard to the sermon and I started to change. I became steadier in my faith.

On a closing note: the earthquake meant my education had to be delayed, so much so that I had to retake my final year at high school. Another answer to prayer came from someone offering to pay my fees for the whole year, and, thankfully, I was able to complete my secondary education. The same people then offered to support me through my nursing training, in the hopes of my being able to fulfil my dream of helping others, especially if another tragedy happens like it did in 2010. Thanks be to God!

## A new quake brewing

As we write this, it is the autumn of 2019. We are now living in a house in Léogâne. Lucie has been at nursing school for over two years and is in her final year. She has had to retake some of her second-year exams, but as of now she cannot do so. Our country is on "lockdown". There are mass protests going on almost every day demanding the stepping down of our President Jovenel Moïse. Our people are sick of suffering under the corruption among our nation's political leaders that has been officially reported now. Of course, there are different opposition parties and groups, each of whom has their own political agenda to agitate for, though none have as yet managed to suggest a constructive alternative plan for changing life in Haiti. We have lived off hearing political promises for too many years. No one believes them anymore or trusts their leaders anymore. It seems that generally, now, people have had enough. They want justice and order, and a fresh start for our country, free from international interference as well. Some think another sort of earthquake is brewing, a political and social earthquake, fraught with so much uncertainty and the potential for yet more violence and destruction and pain. To be sure, if that does happen, it will be the women of Haiti who will suffer most; we always do. Only God can help us, just as he did in 2010.

# CHAPTER 7

# DISASTER: WHAT SURVIVORS THINK, AND HOW BEST TO HELP

### LUC HONORAT

I am very grateful for the invitation to contribute to this book by writing a chapter in which I want more to testify than to teach, as a witness of the earthquake in Haiti; that was definitely a particular kind of trial. Therefore, it is fitting to open this chapter with the words of the Apostle James: "Count it all joy, my brothers, when you meet trials of various kinds, for you know that the testing of your faith produces steadfastness. And let steadfastness have its full effect, that you may be perfect and complete, lacking in nothing" (James 1:2–4, ESV).

I will never forget that day; it was a great testing. Like the words of James and Paul say, when we go through the trial, it tests our faith. Faith comes by hearing, and hearing by the word of God. Faith is the knowledge that God is there for us. Most of the time, God is closer to us than the suit I wear is to me. God is right there for us. This is what I learned so well from our experience of the earthquake. On the one hand, the experience of the earthquake was such a great shock, but on the other hand, because of the awareness of God's mercy that it created among our community, it was, I believe, a precious time.

In this chapter, I will describe what it was like for us to experience a powerful earthquake and the effect it had upon me, and upon the many people I, as a church pastor, had care of. I will also describe the kind of help and assistance we received; what my thoughts, as a Haitian survivor, are of that assistance; and what I feel is needed most for Haiti to move forward toward recovery.

First of all, however, I think it is important to understand that catastrophes like the earthquake do not happen in a vacuum. They take place at a point in the history of a people, to a people who had a life before the catastrophe; and how they lived that life influences the way they respond to and recover from such catastrophes, and how they go on to live their life. In fact, we Haitians probably know more about survival of catastrophes than most of those non-governmental organizations (NGOs) that flooded into our small country to help us in our greatest hour of need. Our history has been one of continuous struggle, and we have learned so many strategies for surviving terrible events. However, that is not to suggest that we have learned how to thrive. My own early years illustrate this point about learning survival, so allow me to share some experiences of those years.

## Early life

I was born and raised in a family of twelve in the mountainous district of Bouvard which rises up to the north of the city of Gonaïves, around 90 miles (150 km) north of the capital, Port-au-Prince (see Figure 7.1). Today it is a barren place and a very poor district of the country.

My father was a Vodou priest for the district. Haitian Vodou (or Voodoo) is a symbiotic religion, combining aspects of the native tribal, animistic religions of the African slaves that were brought in by the Spanish and the French to work the sugar plantations of Haiti, and the Roman Catholicism of their colonizers. Vodou is an official, state-recognized religion along with Catholicism and Protestantism in Haiti today.

There was also an uncle of mine living there. He had a salt pond. So he used to carry salt in his sailboat down to Port-au-Prince, and also to the smaller ports of Grand-Goâve and Petit-Goâve, west of the capital. My uncle eventually got married in

Grand-Goâve and settled there. One day he came to my mother and asked her to give me to him. I was around eight years old at the time. He promised he would look after me and give me a better chance in life, because in Bouvard there was no school and no real future prospects for my life. He said he would treat me like a prince and give me the best education. My mother agreed to this request and so I sailed a seven-day trip to Grand-Goâve with my uncle in his boat.

It so happened that my uncle ran a bakery, as well as a salt storage business in the town. He put me to work as his slave, selling his bread and his salt on the streets of our town. I had to beg him to send me to school. Eventually, I was able to make a deal with my uncle: he could put me to work for him in the bakery in the morning, and then he could send me to school in the evening. I also got my uncle to agree to another deal: he would bring me to see my parents and family every four years. This kind of "slavery" has been very common, and has been widely accepted, in Haiti. It goes under the name of "*restavek*". Only in very recent years has it become a matter of serious civic and social concern.

Each time I would arrive back to my parents' home, my father would prepare a big Vodou ritual. He would go into the bushes and cut off many different kinds of leaf to make a potion, to ensure nothing wrong could happen to me. One time, when I was 17 years old, I remember going back to visit my father. I found my young sister was very sick, and so my father tried to use magic to cure her. He buried my sister in the ground, up to her neck. One day, at 8:30 a.m., I heard the evil spirit say through my sister's own mouth that she would be dead by midday. At midday she died.

That experience was a big turning point in my life. It struck me so deeply. I became so disappointed at the failure of the Vodou of my father to help my sister. I realized that I needed something better than my father had.

When I got back to Grand-Goâve, one Sunday evening I dressed up and decided to go for a walk around the town. I came across a large group of people having a service of worship in the open air. This meeting eventually led to my becoming a Christian. My father thought I had gone crazy. It was his sincere hope that I would succeed him as the Vodou priest where he lived. I also lost most of my friends in the Grand-Goâve area. As the years went on, I still kept in contact with my father and respected him, and he came to respect me as well. During my return visits to my father in Bouvard, I was able to preach the gospel to the population there. Soon I formed a church in Bouvard, and today it is a satellite church to our main one in Grand-Goâve.

In Grand-Goâve, I became an associate pastor in a church for 18 years. During that time, the senior pastor purchased some land in his own name and started a children's home there. I had married, and my wife and I lived there and took care of the children. Then, in October 1992, the senior pastor died. We buried him on Saturday, 19 October 1992. The next day, Sunday, his children started to fight over what to do with their father's land. One of his sons came to my pulpit and announced himself to be a pastor, because he knew that everything belonged to his father. Then on 5 December the deceased pastor's family called me for a meeting at which they showed me all the papers regarding the land their father had bought in his own name. They abruptly announced to me that, being the only surviving relatives, they wanted to sell the church property and to close the church and the children's home. (In Haiti, you do not need to have made a will. If you were a child of the deceased parent then you automatically qualified as a beneficiary of their estate.) I pleaded with them not to do that. I said to them, "The church is not a factory, you cannot close it!" Talking to the family like this made them very mad with me. That evening, they went into the children's home and ordered all of the children and staff to leave. Well, we had nowhere else to go other than to the little house my wife and I owned then. I heard my wife say to the children, "Let's go home". So we did. We took around sixty-six children back to our 1,200 sq ft home – one little house, a shed, and one outside toilet (outside of which every morning we would line up). We also started a school in our home for 150 children. Packed like sardines in a tin, we functioned in these circumstances for ten years, and that time taught me a lot about investing in people.

I had helped a Canadian woman from British Columbia support a Haitian boy going through high school. She had come to Haiti to see the boy she had supported, and she had also seen the circumstances of our home and of the children. In 1996, she invited me to come to Canada, with a view to helping me raise support for our project. As a result of that trip, Heart to Heart in Haiti, a not-for-profit organization, was born. After making several more trips to Canada, I was able to raise enough financial support to purchase some land and to begin to build our own proper children's home. When that project was complete, I made some further trips to Canada and then to Florida, USA, raising more support. Afterwards, I set about building church premises on the land I had purchased. Finally, I was able to build the school premises. Then, just as the whole project – children's home, church, and school – was finished, the earthquake struck. Most of the structures collapsed.

## The earthquake

A momentous day in the memory of all Haitians was 12 January 2010. We will never forget it because we never even dreamed about the things that happened that day. For me personally, that day was a great shock, as I'm sure it was for many others.

Two days before the earthquake, on the Sunday, we had a great service in our church in Grand-Goâve. I also learned that two members of our daughter church, at Fauché, were very sick and in hospital in Léogâne, a city about 20 miles (35 km) west of our capital city, Port-au-Prince. I said I would go to visit them in hospital the next day, Monday. However, that Monday I was very busy. I was invited to some meetings and so I missed the chance of visiting those members. On the following day, Tuesday 12 January, in the late afternoon, I, with a friend, drove in my pickup truck to the hospital in Léogâne with the purpose of visiting the two sick church members.

**Figure 0.1** Collapse of poor quality housing in Port-au-Prince.

**Figure 1.1** A comparison between the response of two new buildings constructed in 2009 to the 2010 earthquake in Haiti. In the foreground is the collapsed three-storey Turgeau hospital. In the background is the 13-storey Digicel phone company building where not a single window cracked.

**Figure 1.2** Town of Saint-Pierre, Martinique, devastated by the Mount Pelée eruption in 1902.

**Figure 3.1** Residential devastation remaining on Bantayan Island, Philippines, three months after the supertyphoon struck.

**Figure 3.2** Lower Ninth Ward, New Orleans, after the floodwaters of Hurricane Katrina subsided.

**Figure 4.1** Dr Linda Mobula's meeting with Dr Kent Brantly after his recovery.

**Figure 4.2** "God is with us in here" scrawled on the wall of a clinic by an Ebola sufferer.

**Figure 5.1** Family photo with Helga Mosey (centre).

**Figure 5.2** An iconic image: the Pan Am 103 cockpit, lying on land at Tundergarth Farm.

**Figure 6.1** Lucie and Marie in Haiti.

**Figure 6.2** Close encounters: life for 50,000 Haitians in an IDP camp in the Delmas area of Port-au-Prince (21 January 2010).

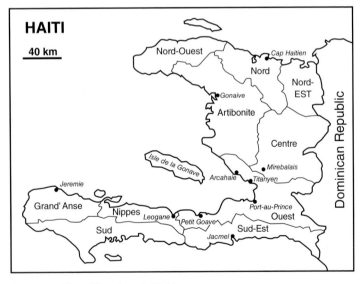

**Figure 7.1** Map of locations in Haiti

**Figure 8.1** New Orleans Baptist Theological Seminary during flooding caused by Hurrican Katrina.

**Figure 8.2** Destruction on the Lower Ninth Ward, New Orleans, after Hurricane Katrina.

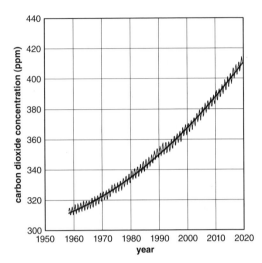

**Figure 9.1** Carbon dioxide levels in the Earth's atmosphere measured at the Mauna Loa observatory on Hawaii from 1958 until the present. The unit of measurement is parts per million (ppm). The black curve shows the seasonal variation, the red curve is the average.

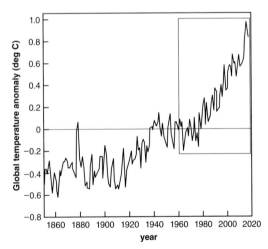

**Figure 9.2** Global temperature anomaly 1850–2017 for land and sea relative to the average global temperature from 1951–1980. The red box is the period of the data shown in Figure 9.1.

When I arrived near to the hospital, my phone rang and I stopped the pickup to answer it. The caller was someone who had been in church with us the previous Sunday; on Tuesday, they had come to visit us in Grand-Goâve and found I was not there. The caller said, "Pastor Luc, I heard you say that you were going to visit Sister Marie, in the hospital in Léogâne. I was told this morning that she has been sent home". So I said that I would go to visit the other member, Pastor Benjamin, instead.[1] However, the caller said that both patients had been sent home from hospital that morning. Just as I was turning the pickup around I heard such a big noise. And it shook! I could not describe what it sounded like because that was the first time I had been through an earthquake. My pickup began to fly.

The first thought that came into my head while all this was happening, was, "This is my time to go home!" I thought to myself that this was the rapture of the church and "I am going to heaven!" In a very short while, however, I realized I wasn't going anywhere. I turned the vehicle engine off and got out to walk along the highway. Buildings were collapsing and people were yelling and carrying terrible injuries. I asked some people what was happening, because I still did not know this was an earthquake. We had never been taught about earthquakes! Only when I saw there was no wind or rain did it dawn upon me that this was not a storm.

The most shocking sight I witnessed was an electricity line snapping and then the whole hospital I had been going to visit my members in collapsing. All inside were killed. It seemed like an angel kept me safe by that one phone call, otherwise I would have certainly been inside that building.

I decided to return to Grand-Goâve. I went back to my vehicle, and as I drove along the route I saw many people who were injured. I put them into my pickup truck and took them to

---

[1] Other than Pastor Luc, all other names have been changed to protect their identity.

the hospital in Petit-Goâve, one of the few hospitals that was still able to function. I then drove back to my home in Grand-Goâve and to the compound. As I approached the gateway into the compound, I was shocked again by the degree of destruction. The whole outside wall of the compound had collapsed and so had most of the buildings. We had a dining hall on the ground floor with a guest house above it. At the time of the earthquake, around 60 of the children were in the dining hall, eating supper. Upstairs there were six girls, cleaning the guest rooms in preparation for a group of Canadian guests who were due to arrive the next day. All the children managed to get out of the hall just seconds before it collapsed. However, everyone else feared that all six girls upstairs must have been killed. The ceilings in this building were all of concrete and all had collapsed.

As I entered the compound, I saw something quite remarkable and shocking. The whole dining block and guest house had collapsed, but there was one place where the roof had come down, leaving a hole. Standing in that hole, her head encased in the steel rebar all bent around her, was one of the cleaning girls, a 14-year-old. When she saw me she cried out, "Papi! Save me!" I ran to pull her out, but I could not move her. My strength went out of me when I found that the concrete roof had collapsed, enveloping her lower body, and the rebar, albeit bent around her, was unyielding. I thought that she must be very severely damaged. I found a large masonry hammer and, with other colleagues, we managed to break the concrete, and we sawed through the rebar sufficiently to lift the girl out. I feared that her lower body must have been crushed, but, to our astonishment, she hardly had a scratch on her. When the rest of the children saw her all covered in white dust, they became very scared and clung to my wife, almost stripping her naked.

The next thing to happen was, when the dust had settled, we asked all the children to look where their bedrooms had been, to see if they could see who was missing. As we were doing this, the rest of the girls who had been cleaning the guest rooms came around the corner from the field that lay outside the back wall of the dining hall and guest rooms. There had been no door in this wall and it had collapsed, yet somehow the girls had found themselves thrown out into the field. Covered in white concrete dust when they approached us, everyone thought they were ghosts at first. No one had thought they could have survived that collapse.

Understandably, all the children of our children's home were very frightened, so I led them onto an open area in front of the ruined dining hall and guest rooms. It so happened that I had a large area there that had been recently concreted over to form a football pitch. We gathered all of the children, safely away from any structures that might collapse with the aftershocks, some of which seemed as strong as the initial tremor. However, not only did the children gather there, so did hundreds of people from Grand-Goâve who were also terrified by the earthquake. A great number of people had gathered outside our compound too. Later that evening, at midnight, there was an enormous aftershock. This terrified everyone and all those outside ran inside my compound.

That patch of ground in the open air became home to hundreds of people for the next four or five weeks. Even many who were Vodou worshippers, including *houngans* (priests) and *mambos* (priestesses) came to be with us there. Since everyone was in shock and was terrified, my focus at first was upon calming people down. To this end, I instituted a programme of regular singing of spiritual songs and the opportunity for prayer. This appeared to have an enormous calming effect upon the people; that is until the aftershocks struck. Then everyone cried out, Christians and Vodou worshippers, "Jesus! Jesus!" That was the name that was upon everyone's lips that first night and for many weeks afterwards. We carried on the practice of singing and prayer through many days and nights.

For many of the Vodou worshippers, they were terrified that the earthquake was ushering in the "last days", the return of Christ and the final judgment, the thought of which terrified them. The terror also provoked within them an urgent desire to ensure they were Christians; so for the first few weeks I had the largest congregations in my church services I had ever had! Until, that is, as the weeks went by and the tremors got less, and people thought that perhaps this was not the time for Christ to return after all, and so they relaxed back into their normal life of practicing Vodou, and my huge congregations gradually began to get smaller.

For us, as Haitians, there was something very special though about those weeks, when we all lived together on the football pitch inside the compound. There was a great sense of unity and of our all being on the same social level. That was the one time, so it seemed to all of us, that Haitians were one. The rich guys, sleeping by the feet of the poor guys. There was no looting or stealing among our people. We ate, and slept, together. We would even make sure a space was kept open when someone needed to go to the toilet. Nevertheless, so traumatized were some of our young people, even 17-year-olds, that they refused to go to the toilet at all during the night.

Some five days after the earthquake – during which time we had made a number of fruitless trips into Port-au-Prince looking for food for our children, who were becoming weaker by the day – to our astonishment a large group of US Marines came ashore near to our church compound. Before landing, they had trawled the internet, attempting to find people to connect with on the ground in Haiti. They found their way to the Grand-Goâve landing from reading my Canadian niece-in-law's online blog that she had been posting since the earthquake. Those Marines made our open compound more secure and they were able to break open our food supplies which had been buried under the rubble. They helped us rescue the two 110 lb (50 kg) bags of rice stored there, and they also rescued our kitchen utensils and pots so we could begin to cook again. The Marines filled both of my empty shipping containers with food and supplies. These supplies we used to feed all those who gathered with us, and those in the town and surrounding villages. As I emptied my containers, so the Marines promised to restock them. So we were really blessed by those Marines, and we shared the food out around the community.

After about three weeks we removed ourselves back into the shade of the school, and people stayed there for the next three or four months. Some people would return to their own homes during the daytime and then go back to the compound for the night when they felt most vulnerable. This was the case especially for those mothers who had children and whose homes had been severely damaged, making sleeping in them unsafe.

Remarkably, we did not have many people who suffered any injuries, and we did not have any instances of very serious illness. Though of course, sleeping in the open air, including when it rained, people did get bad colds. Then, in the October, the cholera epidemic started in Haiti, but again no one in our compound got sick, and we only heard of a handful in the town that went down with the disease.

## What we think and how to help us best

The Haitian people are very resilient. To understand this, we need to get back to the early years of the Haitian slaves. During these years of enormous struggle, Haitians learned how to survive. When the earthquake happened, some people were left with nothing, but I observed that Haitians love to be together, to support one another. I observed that for Haitians being rich is not a matter of money or possessions, it is the people.

## Vodou, faith, and class

When Christopher Columbus first set foot in Haiti, the first thing he did was to place the cross (a crucifix) in the ground. The Spanish colonizers would not permit the slaves to enter into the church; instead, they had to stay outside and look after their master's horse. They said that "the black man" did not have a soul, so they did not need to go to church. Therefore, instead of going to church, the slaves "went back to Africa". By that, I mean they went searching for their African roots, their spirit. Then they created Vodou, as a secretive "marriage" between Vodou and the colonizers' Catholic faith. When the colonizers realized that they needed their slaves to be compliant, they agreed to allow them to come into the Catholic Church. Therefore, Catholicism and Vodou became closely meshed together. The slaves worshipped their Vodou spirits under the guise of communing with the Catholic saints. This is why today, if you travel around Haiti, you will see many Vodou priests. They try very hard to be recognized by the government, so they can get legal recognition for taking services for marriage, funerals, and so on.

Vodou has become the culture of Haiti. I remember one incident when I was a child. My mum had beat me for some reason, and so I ran to my grandmother because she was gentle to me. She went outside the house, late at night, looking for a tree where there was a spirit, because she believed that the spirits could protect me. Another time, one of my cousins told me that as a girl she was used by an evil spirit every night for a period of time, and that led to her losing her virginity.

However, even though taking the above into account, when I heard that American preacher (Revd Pat Robertson) say that the reason for the earthquake striking Haiti was due to Haiti being cursed by the pact with the devil made by the slaves, at Bois Caïman, back in 1791, I did not believe that. To me, the earthquake was like the rains that fall. When the rains fall everyone gets blessed. When the earthquake happened it was a natural catastrophe, and it affected everyone – Catholic, Protestant, Vodou.

What I really love, looking back, was when that aftershock hit us at midnight and everyone called on one name, "Jesus!" All Vodou priest friends I have, they became very humble. They did not call out to their spirits. They called on one name, which is Jesus. Everyone wanted to come to church; they felt safer being closer to Christians. They see that Christians have more love to take care of the people. We have a saying in Haiti, "the dog will never go to the tailor, but you will see the dog by a butcher", because the dog always knows where to get his food. The Vodou worshippers know where to get the love, and to get the food. They know where to feel secure, because they felt that Jesus might be coming, and they do not want to go to hell.

In Haiti, many politicians and upper-class people are into Vodou. To build a good country we need to help each other; yet the politicians and upper class do not want this to happen, because if it did they would not be able to take advantage of people, like they do, to make themselves rich. We never had any government people come to our property to advise us about rebuilding; only a few NGOs do that. For our rebuilding project at Grand-Goâve, we rebuilt to strict standards, and made sure that we did not use concrete for our roofs, but only light materials. I believe if we have another earthquake we will have less damage to our new properties. But there are many poor people in Haiti who cannot build to strict standards. Because they need to live somewhere, they will build whatever they can afford.

## The challenges for Haitians

All pastors and all principals of schools need to teach a new generation about earthquakes, because in my time we did not receive any education about them. Only after the earthquake in 2010 did I learn that we have two large active faults running through our country – one in the south and one in the north. So now, it is our duty to keep a record of the earthquake in 2010 that destroyed Port-au-Prince and killed around 230,000 people.

The way I see it, Haiti cannot be rebuilt without Haitians. I really do appreciate the help that other countries gave to us after the earthquake, but I believe, and I teach my congregation this: we Haitians need to do our part as well. Foreigners may come and tell us to do this and that, but we Haitians need to sit down with them and discuss with them first how we Haitians see what needs to be done. In other words, we Haitians need to take control. I pray for Haitians who love Haiti to bring about change in Haiti after the earthquake. Haitians with a conscience need to sit down together at the table and, with some friends from other countries, discuss what is the best for our country. We should not need the UN MINUSTAH[2] telling us what to do; we should not need NGOs telling us what is best for us. We, as Haitians, should be deciding that ourselves!

We need an example to help us quit fighting among ourselves. This is an area where the Christian Church in Haiti should be leading, by an example, in how to sit down together. However, when it comes to politics, too many Christians refuse to get involved, because they think there is too much corruption involved with politics. They are right as well about that! Some people in Grand-Goâve wanted me to stand for mayor. They said they would help me. I declined their offer, because I knew that if I received money from them, there would come a time when I would be expected to give money to them in return. I guess in some ways, having such convictions does make me a politician of sorts. What I mean is, I love Haiti! Therefore, when I see a person getting away with something criminal; when I see someone hungry; when the mayor does not do what he is supposed to do, I get mad! I challenge them. For this attitude, I have even been threatened lots of times, but that does not trouble me. If you hit me while I was in England, you would have survived. However, if you hit me back in Grand-Goâve, in Haiti, even in front of a gang, they will kill you. This is because not only am I a pastor, I am also a servant for my area.

Therefore, I teach my people to exercise their vote during elections. I invite the candidates to come and speak in our churches, to explain their agendas, and then I encourage my people to vote. I do not tell them what to vote. That is their responsibility. Even so, I know some people who will never vote; and I tell them if they do not vote then someone will vote instead

---

[2] MINUSTAH (*Mission des Nations Unies pour la Stabilisation en Haïti*) is the United Nations' stabilization force that operated in Haiti between 2004 and 2017.

of them. The real tragedy is that we only see our politicians at election time. I wish they would come more often to sit down with us, to ask forgiveness, and to seek reconciliation. But that never happens. The politicians are inaccessible to us here.

So many NGOs, when they come here, do not know how – or simply do not want – to blend in with our culture. They only have enough time to come with their money, to set about their own projects, and then leave. They do not have the time to come and first learn about our way of doing things, which I know may be very frustrating for them if they did take the time. It is important in Haiti to earn respect. Too many NGOs arrive here with their projects and money; they take labourers away from existing employment with the lure of higher wages, and then when they leave the country the Haitian labourers are without work and have no additional skills either. I do not believe that is the best way to help Haiti. Rather, Haitians need time spent on mentoring them and building up their skills, building their confidence so that they may be able to start something for themselves to make a living. I believe it is vitally important to give Haitians responsibility.

# CHAPTER 8

# HOW ONE CHURCH SURVIVED HURRICANE KATRINA

## (AND WHAT THEY LEARNED, WITH THE HELP OF GOD)

### KEN TAYLOR

New Orleans is well known for being flood prone. From the city's inception in 1717, the Mississippi River, the reason the city was located where it is, and its biggest asset, also proved to be one of its biggest liabilities. For over 200 years, until the United States Corps of Engineers built adequate levees, the river at flood stage would often inundate parts of the city with its waters. In recent decades, due to high-quality levees and other flood control measures, the largest river in the USA, running alongside and through New Orleans, has not created major flooding in the city.

Another aspect of flooding episodes in New Orleans is related to the relatively heavy rains that fall here and the fact that much of the city has always been at or below sea level. These areas were swampy and almost always covered with some water. Heavy rains would just deepen the water in these marshy areas. As the city grew and began to expand out of the originally inhabited French Quarter, canals were dug, first to drain these swamps, and later to be conduits for water pumped out of the city by massive mechanical pumping stations. Without these canals and pumping stations, the below-sea-level bowl that is much of the city would be covered with water, especially during heavy rains. Even with this elaborate drainage system, heavy rains can overwhelm the pumping capacity, causing street flooding and worse.

Although the Mississippi River and heavy rains both have caused much flooding over the years, the biggest fear, when it comes to flooding, is the all too real threat of tropical weather moving into the area from the Gulf of Mexico. Hurricanes, tropical storms, and tropical depressions can bring to the city great amounts of rain. Powerful winds can also accompany these storm systems. However, the greatest threat to the city of tropical systems is the surge of water that moves ahead of the storm and with the storm, and can move onto shore, bringing damaging and life-threatening floods. Since New Orleans is at such a low elevation, and since there has been a great loss of protective land between New Orleans and the Gulf of Mexico, these storm surges pose a great danger to the city.

The storm surge from Hurricane Katrina was, in fact, the cause of most of the damage and loss of life that resulted from the 29 August 2005 natural disaster. The storm surge was almost 28 ft at parts of the Mississippi Gulf Coast. Although it was less than this to the west, around New Orleans, the surge was still very significant, causing two major outcomes. First, the rising water from the surge increased greatly the water level in Lake Pontchartrain, bordering New Orleans primarily to the north, and in other waters to the east of the city. These rising waters overtopped some of the lower levees in eastern parts of the city, flooding much of New Orleans East. However, the levees along Lake Pontchartrain, west of the Industrial Canal, were of sufficient height to prevent overtopping. Canals, used to pump rainwater out of the city and into Lake Pontchartrain, were lined with concrete walls to keep pumped rainwater in the canal as it was being pumped into the lake. These walls were also of sufficient height to keep the water from overflowing the canals. A major factor in the flooding of much of the city resulted from waters from the storm-surged, heightened Lake Pontchartrain flowing back toward the city through these canals. As it turned out, the concrete walls lining these canals were not properly supported. Although there were pilings that were supposed to anchor these canal walls securely into the ground, it was later determined that the pilings were not put deep enough into the ground. Some of the pilings were actually in deposits of sand resting beneath the canals. As a result, when the water rose in these canals, the pressure caused the walls to fall outward in a number of locations. From this failure, waters poured into the city until the water level in New Orleans was equal to the water level in the lake. Approximately 80 per cent of New Orleans was flooded with approximately 6–14 ft of water.

I had moved to New Orleans in 1983 to attend New Orleans Baptist Theological Seminary. I also began serving Elysian Fields Avenue Baptist Church as pastor in 1987 after serving on the staff of that church for three years. My wife and I raised four children in the city. Up until 2005, we had tropical weather scares about every other year. Sometimes there would be more than one threat during a hurricane season. My wife and children had evacuated a number of times as we had tropical storm or hurricane watches or warnings. I had never evacuated. A sense of adventure and a sense of needing to stay and help my church and community after the storm always led me to stay in the city when it was tropically threatened. I am not sure if it was adventure or responsibility that was the biggest motivator for me to stay in the city. During these threats, we seldom saw much damage in our community or at our church. Every few storms we might lose electricity for a few hours or for a few days. Occasionally I was able to help some church members, or some neighbours, or at least help clean up lawns that might have a few broken branches scattered about.

There was something different as Hurricane Katrina entered the Gulf of Mexico. At first, the storm was projected to hit Florida. Gradually the projected path began to move closer and closer to New Orleans. Finally, the prediction was that it would make a direct hit on New Orleans. At times while the storm was in the Gulf of Mexico, it was a category 5 hurricane. People began to evacuate the city. For the first time ever, I decided that I would evacuate.

We had planned a church event to honour our oldest church member and to raise some money to make some badly needed repairs on our building. On Sunday 21 August, the last Sunday we met before Katrina hit, we had had a wonderful crowd, lots of visitors, and there was a spirit of excitement as we were engaging upon our efforts to restore our building. As the next Saturday came, the night we were to have our special event, a sense of fear swept over the city with the approach of the ferocious storm. We cancelled the event and cancelled church services for the next morning, 28 August.

## The flood and evacuation

My wife and our 14-year-old twins left New Orleans early on Sunday morning. They drove out at the same time as one of our friends. They drove toward the home of a family member in North Alabama, about 400 miles (640 km) away. Traffic was not bad for them and they made the trip in the usual six hours. I decided that I would leave a little later that day. I wanted to see if we had church members that needed transportation to evacuate New Orleans. I also had a minor repair to make on the roof of our church. During the day, I called around to church members and attendees that might not have a way to evacuate. Most people had the required transportation, but one grandmother and two of her grandchildren that lived with her needed a ride. I made the repairs to a small hole in our church roof. I came home, took a shower, packed three days' worth of clothes (evacuations were not usually for more than three days), loaded just a few other essentials in the car, and headed down to an inner-city neighbourhood and picked up the grandmother and her two grandchildren.

Traffic conditions were not as good when we left the city. The wind was beginning to blow, but the problem was that by now many people had decided to evacuate. Traffic was bumper to bumper, and the trip that should have taken six hours took almost double. Like so many others of our church members and residents of New Orleans, we were now the recipients of the kindness of friends, family, or strangers in many scattered places throughout the USA. This is how the longest evacuation of a large city in America came about.

Katrina began impacting New Orleans early on Monday morning, 29 August, shortly after we arrived at our temporary new home in North Alabama, at my mother's house. Most of our church members, we later found out, had indeed made it out of the city. Winds whipped the city, but the storm's wind fury had lessened somewhat as it hit our location, and the storm had taken a slight eastern track, keeping us out of the most severe wind of Katrina. A church-member couple who had stayed in New Orleans because of a daughter, who could not leave because of her job at a hospital, called us at about 9 a.m. that morning. They lived less than one block from our church and reported that their house was in good condition and that they just had a few tree branches fallen on the ground outside.

During the morning, high water in several canals began exerting pressure on their concrete walls, which the inadequately supported walls were not sufficient for. Sections of the walls of three canals began to fall outward under the water pressure. Millions of gallons of water began to pour out of the breaches. In some of the locations, houses were simply swept away. Houses that were further from the breaches survived the onslaught of water but experienced serious flooding (see Figure 8.1). Our friends who had called us earlier called back to say that water was now coming into their home. They told us they had called the emergency services and that they would soon be rescued. They were in their attic. We at first thought this flooding was limited to their neighbourhood. We were to find out within the next 24 hours that most of the city flooded and that thousands of people were stuck in floodwaters, in their attics, on their roofs, or trying to walk or swim through the water. This couple was eventually able to be rescued by boat, and they made it to a place of safety.

Communication soon became very problematic. Landlines were flooded out and the mobile phone network was very limited. Most mobile phones in the New Orleans area simply did not work. Sometimes people were able to get a few texts out, although it sometimes took hours for them to go through. I was a pastor who knew where few members of his church were and who was able to contact just a small handful of them. I quickly saw how vulnerable we were to this type of situation. We had not adequately prepared for communication with members in an emergency. This was during the infancy of social media, and it was of little benefit to us.

The grandmother who had evacuated with us had three children and several other grandchildren that had been in New Orleans as Katrina approached. She did not know what had happened to them. She spent time looking at the news on TV to see if she might spot any of them. I helped her by searching the Red Cross website to see if any of her family members were registered with that organization. We were able to find one of her sons that way. After a few days, a former staff member at our church, now serving a church in Mississippi, called to check on us. His church was serving as a temporary shelter for Katrina evacuees. He said that he had some children that had attended our church. They told him their grandmother's name. He asked us if we knew of a person by that name. It was the grandmother sitting in my mother's house looking for her family on the news. Soon this family was able to get back together, and they settled in Texas.

During the first few days of the evacuation, Katrina evacuees, including our church members, began to receive acts of kindness and hospitality that still move me to the core when I think about them. My mother's neighbours and church members began bringing food to her home for her new occupants. People bought clothes for us. We quickly learned that the three-day supply of clothes we had brought was not going to do.

Church members moved in with friends and family. One church family was allowed to live in a church Sunday school room for months. Some lived in hotel rooms paid for by the federal government. Some were given homes to live in temporarily. Many, upon their return to New Orleans, were provided with small travel trailers to put on the lawns of their homes while they worked to restore their houses.

## Returning home

It was almost three weeks after 29 August before I could get back into the city. Even then most people were not allowed in. I planned I was going to plead with the soldiers guarding the exit ramps into the city that I was a pastor and that I needed to see my church. It so happened that my vehicle was between two work convoys entering the city and I was waved on through. What I found was a deserted city and neighbourhood (see Figure 8.2). I went to my church and it was damaged, wet, and dark, and I wondered if we could ever be back in our building. The surrounding neighbourhood was devoid of any living soul. No one had returned. About the only living thing I saw was a dog, probably looking for anyone, as was I.

Since old phone numbers were no longer valid, I wrote a letter to my church members, made copies of it, put each in a plastic freezer bag, and went to their flooded and abandoned homes. In the letter I told them where I was staying in Alabama and what my new phone number was. All but two of our church members had flooded residences. I put the letter in a place where I hoped they would see it when they were able to return to check out their flooded mess. As soon as the city started allowing people back in, church members started finding the letters I had left for them. I started receiving phone calls from church members who had evacuated to several different states. Gradually, we began to hear from everyone. Some planned to return as soon as they could, and some would never return to New Orleans to live. By the end of one year, I had heard from or seen all but one child who had been attending. Finally, I was able to determine that he made it out safely too.

Church members and attendees who rented their homes were the slowest returnees. Those who owned their homes had a greater incentive to return; also government grants, to help with the rebuilding process, were made available. We had a lot of children and youth who were attending our church before Katrina. Unless their parents were attending and were homeowners, almost none of them came back within the first two years after the hurricane. Many people in our area not only lost everything they had in the flood, most, if not all, of their friends and family lost everything as well. This left so many that were unable to rely on any help nearby. The kindness and hospitality of people throughout the USA in places to which we evacuated were critically important and are never to be forgotten.

Our church building had some long-standing structural issues before the flooding hit. Our sanctuary, built in 1964, had laminated wooden beams across the ceiling. These beams had deteriorated over the years. With the flood waters that had sat in our building for 18 days and the wind damage the building sustained, it was determined that the building could not be restored. We had no choice but to demolish the structure and decide where to go from there. Just over four months after Katrina hit, we had a few people that had been able to find a place to stay in the city. The couple that had gone to their attic and called us the morning the storm hit offered to let our church meet in their house, which by now had been gutted and cleaned. We met for the first time after the storm on a Sunday in January 2006. We had 24 people show up for that first service. As far as I know, every church member, who had by then come back to New Orleans, was present. I did not yet have a place to stay permanently in the city, since our one-storey home had received 4 ft of water. I would drive six hours to New Orleans each weekend and then drive back to Alabama to be with our 14-year-old twins. In January, my wife had to come back to New Orleans for her job. She would drive back to Alabama on the weekends to be with our children.

About five weeks after the flood, we were able to go to our home and see what we could salvage. Very little could be recovered. Mould had begun to attack almost everything in our wet house. We recovered about seven plastic tubs of material goods. Gone were most of our keepsakes, pictures, clothes, and household furnishings. We were now essentially homeless and had few material goods. However, God helped us and sustained us through this period of time. The generosity of God's people was amazing. By the time our home was gutted, cleaned, rewired, and completed, almost 11 months after the flood, we were able to totally refurnish the house. The church continued to meet, and people were returning very gradually. The couple whose gutted house we were meeting in were ready to begin reconstructing the inside of their home. We needed a place for our church to meet. We had determined that we were not going to be able to rebuild our church building on our property due to new city regulations that required more parking spaces than we had room for on our site.

## Two churches

Gentilly Baptist Church was located slightly over a mile from our Elysian Fields Avenue Baptist Church. The London Avenue Canal, located about a mile from each church, had breached and caused the flooding of both churches and their neighbourhoods. Probably within an hour from the breach, the flood waters approached Gentilly Church. Very quickly, water encompassed its neighbourhood, and 7 ft of water covered the inside of the church's buildings. All furniture, musical instruments, pews, literature, and appliances on the first floors of its buildings were total losses (the first floor in the USA equates with the ground floor in the UK).

Across the street from Gentilly Church, a father came out of his house after the winds of Katrina had died down. It was still morning on 29 August. He surveyed his house and surroundings and saw no major damage. As he was standing outside his house he heard a noise from up the street. As he looked northward, he saw a wall of water pushing toward him. He knew this was serious and that his single-storey home was not safe. He rushed into his house and got everybody outside. He looked across the street and saw the three-storey education building of Gentilly Baptist Church. The family headed there. Finding the door locked, he did what he had to do and broke through the door. His family made it safely into the building and ascended to the upper floors. Over the next few hours, others from the neighbourhood found their way into the safety of this building. There was very little food, but there was a little bottled water in the building. For several days, 17 people waited to be rescued. Some made their way to the roof and were eventually rescued by helicopter. The remaining individuals were evacuated by boats coming through the neighbourhood.

Not only did Gentilly Baptist Church provide a safe haven for dislocated neighbours, this church reached out to our church through Dennis Cole, who had been a member of Gentilly for many years. Through him, Gentilly offered to let Elysian Fields Avenue Baptist Church use a second-floor Sunday school room to have our Sunday services in. Electricity was supposed to be restored by June 2006, and we had our first service at Gentilly Baptist on 11 June.

The electricity had not been restored, so after a terribly hot service in the gutted sanctuary, we went on to meet outside, near the side or the road, until the middle of August. There was some shade, and it was fairly comfortable until August arrived. We were quite a spectacle, worshipping outside in the New Orleans heat. Traffic was still fairly light on the street in front of the church, but quite often a car would slow down or stop to observe or take a picture of the little group gathered in front of a flooded church to worship.

In the early months after Katrina, even though I realized that our church building was a total loss, I was determined that we would build back on the same property and we would continue to be Elysian Fields Avenue Baptist Church. I had poured my life into the ministry of that church, and my ego led my determination to return to that address and have that same church name.

As we experienced the hospitality of Gentilly Baptist Church, my disappointment (it appeared that we would not be able to return to 3515 Elysian Fields Avenue) lessened. In fact, early in 2007, the remaining members of Elysian Fields Avenue Baptist Church voted that we merge with Gentilly Baptist Church. I supported this decision and even supported the aspect of the merger that held that the name of the merged church would still be Gentilly Baptist Church. The assets of the two churches were merged. Even though Elysian Fields had substantially more insurance proceeds, we still felt that it was best to combine our funds. Gentilly had a surviving building, which could be repaired, and Elysian Fields had more money, which could be used for these repairs.

One of the factors that made the merger so attractive was the partnership that Gentilly had established with Arkansas Baptist Convention (ABC)'s Baptist Builders organization. Through this organization, ABC (a part of the Southern Baptist Convention: the largest Protestant denomination in the USA) invested very heavily in the rebuilding of New Orleans after Katrina. Very soon after Katrina struck, disaster relief workers from many different states and organizations began to arrive. ABC started with feeding units, cooking food for residents and for workers. ABC decided that through their Baptist Builders they would make a long-term commitment to stay in New Orleans and help rebuild homes and churches.

ABC's Baptist Builders began looking for a place they could use as a base of operations. Someone suggested Gentilly Baptist Church to them. This was before Elysian Fields had moved to the Gentilly facility and before Gentilly had begun to have Sunday services again. A few members of Gentilly met and had a business meeting. They decided that Elysian Fields could begin having services at Gentilly and that ABC's Baptist Builders could use the church facilities as their base of operations in helping to do rebuild work. Many volunteers began coming our way. Baptist Builders was led by Jackie James. Jackie was a skilled electrician and owned a sign company. God had been leading Jackie and his wife Linda to a deep involvement in missions. This couple made a long-term commitment to New Orleans and they began the process of making Gentilly fit for housing, feeding, and sending out volunteers. ABC was very generous in making money available to rehabilitate parts of our facility to make it volunteer friendly.

The first phase of the work was to equip the second and third floors of our education building so that volunteers could sleep there. On the first floor, where there had been 7 ft of water, much cleaning and restoration was required. A Sunday school room was converted to a shower room. Another room was set up and equipped as a kitchen. Finally, a dining room was placed in another room. It did not take long for the first floor to be completed, and the volunteers began to pour in. Many of the volunteers came from Arkansas, but many others came from elsewhere in the USA and even from other countries.

With the influx of volunteers, Baptist Builders were ready to start. They began sending teams throughout the city, but especially in the neighbourhoods surrounding Gentilly Baptist Church. They received job requests from hundreds of homeowners and from churches as well. From these job requests, teams were assigned to the gutting of houses, the electrical wiring of homes, carpentry, sheet rocking, and painting. Hundreds of homes were worked on. Several churches were also rebuilt. Over a period of about seven years, approximately 10,000 volunteers had stayed at our church, working with Baptist Builders. Large numbers of other volunteers came and worked in our neighbourhood without staying in our facility. Over 1,000 university students from the north-east USA came over a period of years, with InterVarsity Christian Fellowship. They worked on many post-Katrina job sites. Our church members were blessed to be able to serve them while they stayed in our facility.

All of the volunteers were a real encouragement to our church and to our community. Prior to Katrina, the neighbourhood around Gentilly was not very open to the ministry of the church. Evangelistic visits were often not received well at all. However, after Katrina and the host of volunteers that came and ministered to such a large part of our community, the attitude toward our church changed drastically. Within a few years after the recovery ministry began, we could visit a home, mention that we were from Gentilly Baptist Church, and we would receive very warm receptions. Just the presence of the volunteers made a difference to us. When our numbers were very small, and although we might have tended to feel a little sorry for ourselves, having volunteers sit in a worship service with us was a huge encouragement. Hundreds of homes were rebuilt by ABC's Baptist Builders. Groups prayer-walked the community. We even did what we called zone mowing. A group would go down the street with several lawnmowers, mowing almost every lawn in sight. This made lots of friends. A plant nursery from Arkansas donated a truck full of young shrubs. Volunteers went door to door asking our neighbours if they would like to have some of these planted outside their house. Since the salty floodwaters had killed most plants, people were very happy to receive these. Still today, many of these plants can be seen growing in our area. Another company donated a truck full of table and floor lamps. By the time this donation was made, many residents had already bought the basics to restock their homes. Evidently though, not that many had purchased lamps. We started giving these out after church one Sunday. People came out of the church with lamps, using their mobile phones to call their friends and neighbours to alert them of this giveaway. Soon we had a small traffic jam in front of the church. This reminded me so much of how the gospel should spread. When we get the light, we ought to tell others where they can find the light.

The first floor of our education building was the first part of our facility that was fully repaired. This made the education building fully functional to house volunteers. However, the work was growing, and more room was needed for volunteers.

Baptist Builders next tackled the job of restoring our gymnasium. The first floor was totally cleaned out. Showers were built and bunk beds were placed in rooms on the first and second floor. The kitchen was stocked with large commercial-grade appliances. Soon this building was able to house about 200 volunteers. The gym was completed in March 2007. We were now able to move our Sunday worship services into the gym. After moving from the Sunday school room on the second floor of the education building in August 2006 to our gutted sanctuary with no restrooms, heating, or electricity, the move to the gym was met with great joy by our members and volunteers.

Our sanctuary was the last of our buildings to be restored; the reasons being we already had a place to meet, with the gym being finished, and we did not want to take a lot of volunteers away from the job of putting people back into their homes. Finally, though, it was time to finish our sanctuary. Some volunteers with good construction skills came and did what they could. Then we hired a contractor, using some of our insurance money. In November 2009, we finally had our sanctuary pretty much completed. Our new chairs were not in yet, but we did not mind sitting on folding chairs. In early 2010, the sanctuary was fully furnished. We had a day of dedication for it. We invited those who had been a part of the recovery process from the time of the flood. It was a great day of celebration. One of the individuals who had found shelter in our education building on the day of the flood even came and shared her testimony of how God was with her in the flood.

## Lessons learned

Many lessons come out of a disaster. The one I value most is learning through experience that God is with us before, during, and after the storm. He does not abandon us, and he provides for our needs. Our church learned the importance of preparing for a disaster. After a disaster happens is not the time to begin preparing. We also learned the importance of community. Loss of community is painful, but God provides community for us. We must strive to maintain a healthy community.

Our church has come to see the crucial importance of partnerships. This is a lesson that cannot be minimized. Many groups, organizations, and individuals partnered with us. The impact of the partnership with ABC's Baptist Builders cannot be overstated. I want to mention one other partnership. Rosebower Baptist Church is in Paducah, Kentucky. This church heard of our need shortly after Katrina. Their members came down several times to help clean out the church. In autumn 2007, the church asked if they could come and do a community party on our church grounds. They came with almost 100 members and prepared a feast for the community and activities to go along with the food. Our community responded in great numbers. It was like a new beginning for our church. God provided wonderful weather, and our neighbours were truly impacted that some people would do something like this for them. Through this partnership, we touched our neighbours like we had never done before.

The recovery process was difficult and sometimes all too slow. We lost a lot of church members. Some eventually came back, and some never came back. We truly learned the truth of 2 Corinthians 12:7–10 (ESV):

> So to keep me from becoming conceited because of the surpassing greatness of the revelations, a thorn was given me in the flesh, a messenger of Satan to harass me, to keep me from becoming conceited. Three times I pleaded with the Lord about this, that it should leave me. But he said to me, "My grace is sufficient for you, for my power is made perfect in weakness". Therefore I will boast all the more gladly of my weaknesses, so that the power of Christ may rest upon me. For the sake of Christ, then, I am content with weaknesses, insults, hardships, persecutions, and calamities. For when I am weak, then I am strong.

We were very weak, painfully weak at times, after the devastation of Katrina. However, we found the words of Christ to Paul absolutely true, that Christ will demonstrate his strength in our times of weakness. In our trials and difficulties, Christ was glorified. I would never want to go through something like Katrina again, but I would not give up the blessings that God has brought to us after Katrina for any amount.[1]

---

[1] Some suggestions for further reading: Jamie Aten, *A Walking Disaster: What Surviving Katrina and Cancer Taught Me About Faith and Resilience* (West Conshohocken, PA: Templeton Press, 2019); Jamie Aten and David M. Boan, *Disaster Ministry Handbook* (Downers Grove, IL: InterVarsity Press, 2015); Lisa R. Baker and Loretta A. Cormier, *Disaster and Vulnerable Populations: Evidence-Based Practice for the Helping Professions* (New York: Springer Publishing, 2015); Paul Blom, *God in the Raging Waters: Stories of Love and Service Following Hurricanes Katrina and Rita* (Minneapolis, MN: Augsburg Fortress Publishers, 2006); Douglas Brinkley, *The Great Deluge: Hurricane Katrina, New Orleans, and the Mississippi Gulf Coast* (New York: HarperCollins, 2006); Bruce Lee Smith, *Soul Storm: Finding God Amidst Disaster: Reflections from a Hurricane Katrina Survivor* (New Orleans, LA: Pelican Publishing, 2006).

# CHAPTER 9

# CLIMATE CHANGE: A DISASTER IN PROGRESS

## HUGH ROLLINSON

> When your house is on fire you don't sit around and talk
> about how nice you can rebuild it once you put out the fire.
> If your house is on fire you run outside.[1]

**C**limate change is upon us and is here to stay. For some in the West it is now a "Climate Emergency". School children across the globe are striking and missing classes in order to call attention to both this emergency and the lack of action from those with political power. How seriously should we take this "threat"? Do the younger generation see things with a greater clarity than those of us who are older?

According to NASA's Goddard Institute for Space Studies, the average global temperature on Earth has increased by about 0.8°C since 1880 and two-thirds of this warming has occurred since 1975.[2] Globally the effects of climate change are felt through differential water availability, storms, flooding, increased soil erosion, drought and related forest fires, and the associated impacts of these processes on food security, human health, migration, displacement, and conflict. Rising sea levels will impact on coastal communities and small island nations. Some

---

[1] Greta Thunberg, *No One is Too Small to Make a Difference* (London: Penguin, 2019), p. 32.

[2] NASA: https://www.giss.nasa.gov/ (last viewed 10 February 2020).

estimates suggest that we will reach dangerous levels of warming within 20–30 years.

This chapter, from an Earth scientist interested in Earth systems, considers the current scientific evidence for climate change and the manner in which it has been induced by human activity. It will then discuss the impacts of climate change on human society and emphasize the urgency to act which this forces upon us. Finally, it leads to a consideration of an appropriate Christian and biblical response. The chapter will argue that climate change is an issue which is not theologically or morally neutral, and that Christian theology has much to say about our attitude to the natural world, including climate change. Further, the chapter argues that the Christian church as God's agent in society should be active in seeking to mitigate the impacts of climate change.

## Listen to the science

In 1958, the scientist Charles Keeling began to record the levels of carbon dioxide in the Earth's atmosphere. His recording station was high on Hawaii's extinct volcano, Mauna Loa, far from any areas of industrial pollution. His work continues today and has become the longest-running direct record of atmospheric carbon dioxide concentrations. The results plotted as changing concentrations over time have become known as the Keeling curve and show that the concentrations of carbon dioxide in the Earth's atmosphere have increased by 32 per cent in 60 years (see Figure 9.1).

Prior to this time, carbon dioxide levels had not changed significantly for more than 800,000 years, indicating that what is currently happening to the Earth is anomalous. The most obvious explanation for the increase in atmospheric carbon dioxide is the modern burning of the fossil fuels – oil, coal, and gas – since carbon dioxide is one of the main combustion products of this process.

Carbon dioxide is what is known as a greenhouse gas. This means that its presence in the Earth's atmosphere causes it to trap heat – a phenomenon that has been known since the early

1800s. The net effect is that the heat radiated from the Sun to Earth cannot escape the Earth as easily as it has done in the past because now the Earth has a thicker "blanket" around it of carbon dioxide gas which is causing the planet to warm. It is now well established that as global carbon dioxide levels have increased, so have average global temperatures, and that the two phenomena are interconnected. The direct measurement of average global temperatures has been recorded since the mid-1800s, and when the results are plotted on a graph it can be seen that the global average temperature curve is flat until the year 1900, shows a gentle increase from 1900–1960, and then rises steeply after 1960. This curve with its distinctive shape has been dubbed the "hockey stick" curve, a term popularized by Al Gore in his film and book *An Inconvenient Truth*. Unless the world reduces its emissions of greenhouse carbon dioxide, then global average temperatures will continue to increase. There is therefore an urgent need to curb greenhouse gas emissions, which means in practice massively reducing our dependency on fossil fuels.

The logical steps in this argument therefore are:

- the levels of greenhouse gases in the atmosphere, in particular carbon dioxide, are increasing;
- this is because of the burning of carbon, as fossil fuels – oil, gas, coal;
- global average temperatures are increasing because of the increased levels of greenhouse gases in the atmosphere;
- global warming is caused primarily by human activity (the burning of fossil fuels);
- global warming is the principal cause of climate change.

## Climate science is not fake news

Over recent years there have been a number of public figures who have denied the link between the burning of fossil fuels and global warming. The most common argument is that the extremes of climate that we see are the product of natural climate cycles involving, among other things, the normal variation in solar activity. Some have suggested that there is a lack of consensus among climate scientists such that their results cannot be trusted, and others that scientists stand to gain financially from their "scaremongering" over future climate change.

As the scientific evidence builds, these proposals look increasingly improbable. The causes of climate change and the resultant global warming have been the concern of the United Nations Intergovernmental Panel for Climate Change (IPCC) – a body of hundreds of well-regarded scientists from all over the world. It is their science which feeds into the policy discussions of the United Nations, and they regularly publish assessment reports, the most recent of which was in 2018. This huge volume of scientific work compiled by scientists working from across the globe shows that climate change as a result of global warming is real. It may well be that a very small percentage of the change observed is due to natural climate cycles, but the major effect, probably more than 95 per cent, is due to global warming. Further, whereas there have been climate anomalies in the past, such as the Little Ice Age in Britain in the Middle Ages, it is now known that these effects were localized. The important result of modern climate research is that the impacts of global warming are indeed global. This is different from anything recorded in the recent past and is significant.

On a more positive note, it has been argued that the effects of global warming will bring beneficial changes to those of us who live in temperate climates, such as warmer summers and the ability to grow new crops. However, this is to misrepresent the science, because in reality the effects of global warming on temperate European climates is to introduce more chaotic and generally wetter weather patterns into these areas. Others have suggested that we do not need to be worried about climate change because we can mitigate against it using new technologies. While it is true that new technologies are being introduced to reduce carbon dioxide emissions, this is only a solution for rich countries. As will be discussed below, climate change exacerbates inequity and it will be the poor and disadvantaged nations that will not be able to respond easily in this way.

It is interesting to note the origin of the opposition to the findings of climate science, for much of it comes from those who are linked to either the fossil fuel industries or the automobile industry. These groups clearly have a vested economic interest in the subject, and use their power and their wealth to discredit the science. However, the views of climate deniers are becoming increasingly untenable as the weight of scientific opinion now supports the view that climate change is happening because of global warming, which in turn is a result of the burning of fossil fuels. An indication of this is the work of William Ripple and others who, together with an extraordinary number of other scientists (11,258 scientists from 153 countries), are reporting significant indicators of a changing global climate.

Accepting responsibility for climate change is a subject less frequently discussed. However, professors Partha Dasgupta and Veerabhadran Ramanathan point out that it is 1 billion people, mostly in the global north, who are responsible for 50 per cent of greenhouse gas emissions, a further 3 billion people are responsible for 45 per cent of emissions, while the remaining 3 billion, a group who do not have access to affordable fossil fuels, are responsible for only 5 per cent of emissions.[3] All nations will be affected by climate change, but the wealthy Western nations will survive its impact better through their ability to "buy" temporary solutions to the problem. It is the 3 billion people who are responsible for only 5 per cent of greenhouse gas emissions who will experience the worst consequences, and it is to these consequences or impacts that we now turn.

---

[3] P. Dasgupta and V. Ramanathan (2014) "Pursuit of the common good", Science, Vol. 345, Iss. 6203.

## Climate change is a matter of social justice

There are three major impacts of global warming, each of which will disproportionately affect the poor.

## The oceans are warming

This is a slow process. It takes several decades for the surface waters of the oceans to warm. This, however, is a problem, because if the oceans warm slowly they will also cool slowly, meaning that even if the causes of a warming Earth ceased today the effects would still last for several decades. There are two major outcomes of a warming ocean. One is that the behaviour of living organisms in the sea will change. Rising ocean surface temperatures will impact fishing industries, as fish stocks will migrate to cooler waters. And yet, fish is a major source of nutrition in many parts of the developing world. A second is that in a warming ocean a greater volume of seawater will evaporate, causing an increased volume and intensity of precipitation, leading to more severe storms, hurricanes, and the associated flooding.

## Drought is becoming more common

Global temperatures are not rising evenly, and in some continental areas they are rising more rapidly than the global average. As rainfall patterns shift, some areas will experience more frequent drought and encroaching desertification. Further, rainfall patterns will become more erratic, rainy seasons will become shorter, and there will be an increased likelihood of forest fires. The major impact of reduced rainfall and higher evaporation from the land will be in the agricultural sector. In particular, it will be felt in those parts of the world where the agriculture is rain-fed and will lead to lower agricultural productivity for both cash crops and domestic crops. There are also other industrial ramifications of a reduction in rainfall – in the energy sector where a country depends on hydroelectric power and on manufacturing, as well as the implications for sanitation and health.

## The ice caps are melting

Meltwater from the polar ice caps and glaciers is increasing the volume of water in the oceans. This is giving rise to a small but measurable rise in sea level. Although a rise in sea level of a few tens of centimetres may seem insignificant, it will impact coastal communities and ocean islands where the shoreline is very gently sloping and can lead to a significant incursion of the sea. This process is already impacting the small island nations of the Pacific Ocean, and when sea-level rise is accentuated with storm surges, the results are devastating. Seawater incursion into coastal areas also impacts their potential for agriculture as their fresh groundwater supplies are polluted by seawater. A further impact is that the density difference between cold freshwater from melting ice and saline seawater in the oceans has the power to change the patterns of ocean circulation, which in turn further influence global weather patterns.

## "Our house is on fire!"

For many years the discussion of global warming has centred around keeping the mean global temperature from rising 2°C above pre-industrial levels, that is the era before global warming in the early 1900s. This 2°C threshold was perceived as the point beyond which there would be little chance of a return to the levels of the late twentieth century. More recently, the 2015 Paris Climate Accord revised this view and said that it was necessary to hold the increase in the global average temperature to *well below* 2°C above pre-industrial levels, and that efforts should be made to limit the temperature increase to 1.5°C, as this would significantly reduce the risks and impacts of climate change. In other words, the United Nations agreement implies that even 2°C of warming is too dangerous and we would be better to set a lower, safer limit. This has been reinforced by recent scientific studies which show that if global warming is not limited to 1.5°C, an additional 1.5 billion people will be exposed to dangerous heat extremes.

Recent data from the United States National Oceanic and Atmospheric Administration (NOAA) indicate that "since the start of the twenty-first century, the annual global temperature record has been broken five times", and "from 1900 to 1980 a new temperature record was set on average every 13.5 years [the change in average global temperature is shown in Figure 9.2]. However, since 1981 the interval between new temperature records being broken has decreased to every 3 years".[4] It is this speed at which global warming is increasing which is the subject of much current concern. Atmospheric scientists use mathematical models to predict how temperatures might change in the future. These models are hugely complex but a recent model from a group at Oxford University predicted that the 1.5°C threshold would be reached in as little as 22 years from 2017.[5] A separate research group made the same point and argued that the combined effects of rising carbon dioxide emissions, declining air quality due to pollution, and the natural cycles of climate systems could combine to hit the 1.5°C threshold by 2030, 10 years earlier than that predicted recently by the Intergovernmental Panel on Climate Change.[6]

A further complexity that has been reported recently is that methane levels are also rising faster than previously predicted. The concentrations of methane are low in the Earth's atmosphere but they are 28 times more efficient at trapping global heat

---

[4] R. Lindsey and L. Dahlman, *Climate Change: Global Temperature*, NOAA: https://www.climate.gov/news-features/understanding-climate/climate-change-global-temperature (last viewed 29 January 2020).

[5] Leach et al. (2018) "Current level and rate of warming determine emissions budgets under ambitious mitigation", Nature Geoscience, Vol. 11, pp. 574–79.

[6] Ibid.

emissions than carbon dioxide, and so they have a major impact on global warming, making them the second most toxic global warming gas.[7]

Taking these concerns together, it is clear with the impacts of global warming that the time available for adaptation and mitigation is short – a few decades at most, and likely within the lifetime of those reading this chapter: and most certainly their children. Worryingly, the few prophetic voices warning of our impending danger are not coming from those who govern our nations. Instead, they are coming from a most unexpected quarter – a Swedish schoolgirl blessed with Asperger's syndrome and an ability to see the stark future clearly. Greta Thunberg has moved from sitting outside the Swedish Parliament every Friday, initially on her own; to leading schoolchildren across Europe in a school strike about climate change; to making presentations to world leaders at the World Economic Forum at Davos, the United Nations, and the UK parliament. In addition to this we have the voice of the very well-regarded television naturalist Sir David Attenborough, whose TV presence has the power to capture public attention. However, we may ask, where is the Christian prophetic voice? What does the Christian church have to say about this subject?

## A Christian response to climate change

In his classic paper of 1967 entitled "The Historical Roots of our Ecological Crisis", Lynn White Jr argued that the present ecological crisis, or in our terms the climate crisis, is the product

---

[7] E. G. Nisbet, M. R. Manning, E. J. Dlugokencky, R. E. Fisher, D. Lowry, S. E. Michel et al. (2019) "Very strong atmospheric methane growth in the 4 years 2014–2017: Implications for the Paris Agreement", Global Biogeochemical Cycles, Vol. 33, Iss. 3, pp. 318–42. https://doi.org /10.1029/2018GB006009

of a Christian world view in which God has given us dominion over the Earth. If this were the case, "Christianity bears a huge burden of guilt" for the ecological crisis. White Jr concludes that "since the roots of our trouble are largely religious, the remedy must also be essentially religious, whether we call it that or not".[8] White is probably not completely accurate in his analysis of the problem because there are also the pressures of secular business interests which played an important role in environmental degradation. Nevertheless, there are Christians who advocate the "dominion view" over nature and argue that the Bible gives us a mandate for using the land for our own needs and that we can use nature as we choose. In fact, it has been argued that God *wants* us to use the resources of our world for our own prosperity (see for example Genesis 1:26). This view, however, ignores the fact that this mandate comes from God himself, and neglects to recognize that he is the owner of the planet and that we are merely his tenants. That being the case, our relationship with God's creation carries with it a high degree of responsibility.

Linked to the dominion view, but separate from it, is the dualistic idea that matter, including the natural world, is fundamentally evil and what really is significant is "the spiritual". Put another way, it is not the here and now that is important, it is securing our eternal destiny that matters. According to this viewpoint, we need to be liberated from this natural world to live in the better spiritual world. Some Christians have used a verse such as 2 Peter 3:10 to justify this argument. In this text, Peter is apparently speaking of the world being burned up before the day of the Lord comes. However, this interpretation can be challenged on two grounds. First, on linguistic grounds the text is better translated "the earth and all its works *will be disclosed*", indicating that on the day of the Lord everything will be tested

---

[8] Lynn White Jr (1967) "The historical roots of our ecological crisis", Science, Vol. 155, Iss. 3767, pp. 1203–07.

by fire and purified, but not completely destroyed. Second, theologically, the passage makes more sense when it is seen in the context of God's long-term purpose for the Earth which is to restore and renew it. Nevertheless, it is easy to see how the outworking of the dominion and dualistic philosophies can lead to the wrong sort of practice in which we believe we can do what we like with the natural world because ultimately it is of no value and one day will be destroyed.

There is, however, a third way, supported by many Christians, and is the view advocated in this chapter. This is the stewardship view. Proponents of this view argue that the Bible promotes our caring for the Earth as a sacred duty, that God wants us as humans to protect the Earth and its resources, and not to rule over it for our own selfish ends. This view was recently reinforced by Pope Francis in his encyclical *Laudato Si*. He argued that it is humankind's sacred duty to be stewards of the Earth, to protect its resources, and to "till and keep the garden of the world".[9] In this chapter, therefore, the stewardship view is advocated as a proper understanding of biblical teaching on the relationship between humankind and the Earth and its resources. In the early chapters of Genesis it is clear that God's creation is good and has value. Some might argue that this all changed at the fall and now creation is no longer good. However, it is clear that in the incarnation of Jesus, God reaffirms the goodness of his creation (see John 1:14, in which John shows how the Word [Jesus] became flesh and made his dwelling among us; and 1 Corinthians 15:45, in which Paul describes Jesus as the last, that is the new, Adam). This means that our attitude to the natural world must be one of stewardship, not one of contempt and exploitation. This is because God's creation belongs to God and not us. God has given us the land to use for our needs but it is still the object of his tender care. He has given us the use of the

---

[9] Pope Francis, Encyclical Letter, *Laudato Si* of the Holy Father Francis on care for our common home (2015).

natural world but we still have a moral responsibility for all of life. This means that our human vocation is to care for the place in which God has put us, and this must involve us in working to limit and reduce the effects of climate change.

Much of the logic for creation care stems from the Old Testament and starts with the creation mandate in the early chapters of Genesis and the rules for rural life in a semi-arid climate. There follows the warnings of the Hebrew prophets, and professor Hillary Marlow in her discussion of "Justice for all the Earth" draws attention to prophetic writings that speak about justice for the land. Using Micah 6 as an example, she states that "the prophet Micah has seen an inextricable link between the way in which people worship God, their treatment of other human beings and the welfare and productivity of their lands". Using other examples from Isaiah, Amos, and Hosea, it is clear that in the Hebrew mind "the world is an interconnected whole, which we ignore at our peril". [10] Similarly, professor Michael Northcott, in his book *The Environment and Christian Ethics*, shows that in the Old Testament nature is the product of an imposition of divine order on the raging forces of the cosmos. It is characterized by a divinely given order and an equilibrium which has a deep moral, social, and spiritual significance. While nature is a divine gift and not to be worshipped, the true worship of Yahweh (a Hebrew name for God) is linked to a respect for the natural order, and that, as is indicated in Psalm 150, all parts of the natural order have a moral duty to worship the Creator. However, it is possible to see the mandate for creation care as expressed in the Old Testament as one of *duty* – a concept which does not play very well in today's society. For this reason, it is helpful to turn to New Testament teaching on this subject.

---

[10] Hillary Marlow (2009) "Justice for all the earth: Society, ecology and the biblical prophets" in Robert S. White (ed.), *Creation in Crisis: Christian Perspectives on Sustainability* (London: SPCK, 2009), p. 197.

## Climate change and kingdom theology

In the New Testament, the subject of restoration – a theme common also in Old Testament prophecies – comes much more to the fore. In particular it does so in the context of the theme of the coming of the kingdom of God. Here, therefore, it is proposed that a Christian understanding of God's kingdom is central to a theology of the natural world. It is suggested that working against climate change is the work of the kingdom, which is highly relevant to bringing in God's new kingdom. Thus, it is argued that the resurrection of Jesus represents a new beginning and is the inauguration of God's new kingdom. In this way, the resurrection of Jesus is the pivotal doctrine of Christianity. In relation to the Hebrew understanding of the created order, it is God's vindication of his creation. The resurrection therefore reaffirms the fundamental goodness and harmony of the created order. In the resurrection, God is renewing his broken world and is providing the basis for the transformation and redemption of the alienation that exists between God and his world stemming from the fall. This alienation was total and included not only the rift between God and humanity, but between humans and non-humans, and between humans and their environment. This highlights the power of the resurrection of Jesus in as much as it inaugurates the restoration of the whole created order. It forms the basis for a Christian hope in an era of an uncertain climate future.

These ideas are well articulated by Tom Wright who has argued, in his book *Creation, Power and Truth*, that God's creation and his new creation are the basis for revolutionary good news. This news includes the message that creation is good, the God who made it is good, and that this same God will one day rescue creation from corruption and decay. The Christian doctrine of the incarnation enriches this view. Since Jesus is the one who came and "dwelled among us", this validates the importance of the natural world and we who are part of it. We see God incarnate transforming from within, not just broken lives but the disorder of the whole of a fallen creation.

Wright continues, arguing that, seen in this way, God's saving purpose is not to rescue people *out of* his world but to *renew creation itself.* Jesus is not one who rescues us *from* creation, but one who *rescues creation* and us with it. Judgment is not the demolition of the created order but the putting to rights of the Creator's good world. Underpinning this view is the belief that there is an organic harmony between creation and salvation. While it is commonplace to acknowledge that it is the same God who is Creator and Redeemer, we do not always see the close association between salvation and the natural world. However, the Apostle Paul is explicit in writing, "in him [Jesus] *all things* were created, in heaven and on earth, visible and invisible, whether thrones or dominions or rulers or authorities – all things were created through him and for him. And he is before all things, *and in him all things hold together*" (Colossians 1:16–17, ESV, emphasis added). From this, we learn that salvation is not a purely individualistic matter: it affects the whole of creation. Just as God created everything, so God in Jesus now holds the whole created order together. For this reason, working in the way God intends us to adapt to and mitigate the effects of climate change is the work of the kingdom.

Mark Clavier, in his discussion of the role of Christian ministry, extends this argument and shows that God saved us *for* his creation. He states that:

> The mission of the church isn't separate and compartmentalised from the world within which it is conducted; it includes that world every bit as much as it includes the people of that world… our ministry is less like a rescue mission than a reclamation project – the rescuing has already been accomplished in Christ.[11]

---

[11] Mark Clavier, *Stewards of God's Delight* (Eugene, OR: Cascade Books, 2016), p. 11.

## Climate change action

Any discussion of climate change is never far from asking the question – so what should we be doing about climate change? As has been shown in the section above, there is a theological imperative for Christians to do something about climate change – motivated as we are to see God's kingdom come on Earth. A major strand in this thinking is that God loves his creation and his work is to rescue, restore, and redeem his creation. It is not to be "burned up" and destroyed but rather restored and made new. Below, four possible areas for action are identified.

## We need an appropriate theology

What we think matters. It governs the way we live. So the way in which we understand creation and God's view of creation will colour our lifestyle. Thus we need a right theology of the natural world. This may sound academic and dry, but when played out in practice it is the heart of the coming of God's kingdom. If we accept the fact that God cares for his creation and intends to renew it, as discussed above, then the Christian church can be seen as God's agent in bringing in the new creation through the actions of creation care. We are participating in the healing work of the Creator, but in order for us to do this we must "get our head straight", we must genuinely believe that it is what we are called to do.

What we think also governs what we say. Katharine Hayhoe, a prominent Christian climate scientist in the USA has said, when asked what we should do about climate change: talk about it.[12] As we talk about climate change with those around us, we can raise an awareness that this is a kingdom issue and something that demands action from all Christians.

---

[12] See for example https://www.ted.com/talks/katharine_hayhoe_the_most_important_thing_you_can_do_to_fight_climate_change_talk_about_it?language=en (last viewed 29 January 2020).

## Climate change is a moral issue

The fact that climate change is a moral issue was brought home to me through the writings of a fellow Earth scientist who had followed some of the early United Nations climate change negotiations as a representative of a climate action group. From his observations, he argued that the central issue of climate change is not predominantly a scientific nor indeed a political one but that it is a moral issue. In any international negotiation there will be parties who have a vested interest in denying climate change because of the impact it will have on their industry or the economy of their country. For them, climate action will decrease their profit margin, and so they will take steps to negate the science of climate change. Unfortunately, these groups also have great power to lobby and persuade governments. We must not let the truth of the science be distorted by those who seek to profit by continued high levels of carbon dioxide emissions.

## Global action

At a national and international level, it is important for us to challenge the actions of our respective governments. Major change will only come through policy change, and yet when electoral success supersedes the longer-term future this view must be questioned. We can make a difference by supporting those political groups who are committed to enacting policies that will reduce and mitigate the effects of climate change. In addition, those few with influence in the world of politics may also be able to bring about change through the regular gatherings of the United Nations where these matters are discussed.

## Local action

Individual and local action in response to climate change will vary. Some churches may wish to participate in the "eco-church" movement. Other more individual actions include the monitoring of our personal carbon footprint using an online carbon footprint calculator.

## Conclusion

A number of authors have drawn attention to the fact that religious groups have the power to change social values and even the attitudes of their governments. This is because religious groups have a sense of community within which it is possible to create the power to motivate their followers to action. This motivation also derives from shared principles, so when an issue which has perceived ethical implications relates to social justice and implicates a consumption-driven lifestyle, then there is common ground for taking up the cause. If, therefore, faith groups can be persuaded of the dangers of climate change, they have the potential to act against it. An example of this is the papal encyclical *Laudato Si* and the power this document has had in the Roman Catholic Church globally to bring awareness of the issues of climate change. This is where we can find hope.

In contrast, even though the Protestant Church has also come out strongly in favour of action against climate change through the influential Lausanne Movement, there has been no unified response from major denominational leaders (see Bell and White, *Creation Care and the Gospel: Reconsidering the Mission of the Church*). In part, this may be attributed to a lack of a unified and pervasive theology of the natural world. Nevertheless, there is hope because there is an appropriate theology of the natural world – a powerful theology based upon the coming of God's kingdom. It is only that this theology needs to become more widely known and better articulated. This would mean that small actions taken in faith-based communities worldwide can have a significant impact in stemming and even reversing the current trends caused by climate change.

# CHAPTER 10

# COVID-19 PANDEMIC: A CHRISTIAN PERSPECTIVE

## ROBERT WHITE AND ROGER ABBOTT

n December 2019, it became evident that a new respiratory virus called COVID-19 had jumped from animals into an unprepared and vulnerable human population. Within weeks, the virus had spread around the world, infecting many and disproportionately killing older people and those with other underlying medical conditions. Drastic measures of social distancing and isolation were put in place by many governments in a desperate attempt to stem its spread. We, the authors, have family members who have caught COVID-19, others who have underlying health problems, are elderly, or are working on the front line of the caring and National Health Services. So, as we write, we share in the anxieties and fears created by this aggressive virus.

However, as committed Christians, we also share in the desire and need to demonstrate compassion and to offer, wherever we can, practical assistance to our "neighbours" – as defined by Jesus – that is, not just the folk "next door" (Luke 10:29–37). We discuss here our conviction, rooted in Scripture, that both Christian theology and practice as well as medicine and science have valuable contributions to offer those caught up in a global pandemic.

## The nature of viruses

Viruses are not living organisms in their own right: they are simply sections of genetic material (DNA or RNA) in tiny packages which infect cells within a host. They then use the host cell's molecular processes parasitically to manufacture many more copies of themselves. Then they infect still more cells. Without transmission to another organism, viral infections die out. That is why isolation and social distancing are effective measures implemented around the world in order to slow down or stop the spread of the COVID-19 virus. We should also recognize that while COVID-19 is pathogenic to humans, there are many other viruses that are beneficial, and indeed essential, to life, including those that destroy some harmful bacteria that don't respond to antibiotics.[1] Most of the problems arise when viruses jump from one species to another that is not adapted to them.

At the time of writing, there is no tested and licensed antiviral drug for COVID-19. If a patient is to survive the infection, he or she has to develop immunity within themselves to render the virus ineffective. The majority of patients manage to do just that, but for the sickest minority, the best care that medical facilities can provide is to keep the person alive sufficiently long to give them a chance to develop immunity themselves. COVID-19 often attacks the lungs, which is why giving oxygen through a mask, or in more severe cases by supplementing lung function with a ventilator, helps to keep the oxygen level at the right level within a patient's blood.

In the longer term, the way to beat the fatal consequences of a virus such as COVID-19 is through widespread vaccination. A vaccine works by injecting an inactive form of the specific virus, or part of it, which doesn't cause the disease, but allows the body to generate immunity to it. A spectacular success story of global vaccination concerns the naturally occurring smallpox virus. Smallpox has been present in the human population since at least the third century BC, and has been found in Egyptian mummies.

---

[1] Marilyn J. Roossinck (2015) "Move over, bacteria! Viruses make their mark as mutualistic microbial symbionts", Journal of Virology, Vol. 89, pp. 6532–35. doi:10.1128/JVI.02974-14.

Those who contracted it had a 30 per cent chance of dying. In the twentieth century, smallpox killed up to 300 million people. But by 1977, it had been totally eradicated from the world, thanks to global vaccination.[2]

One characteristic of viruses is their ability to mutate rapidly, which makes it difficult to create a vaccine with long-term effectiveness. Influenza, or the common flu, is one such example. Because the main winter flu seasons occur six months apart in the northern and southern hemispheres, vaccines made for one hemisphere may not subsequently be effective in the other hemisphere because the virus has changed: so the genetic make-up of flu viruses has to be monitored continually across the globe. In 1918, no flu vaccine was available for what became known as the "Spanish flu" and an estimated 50 million people died.[3] Even with modern medical understanding, flu still kills many people. In England and Wales alone in the 2014–15 winter, there were an additional 16,415 deaths from flu.[4]

Some of the most virulent and dangerous viruses are those that have crossed from animals to humans. The lack of previous exposure in the human population often renders such viruses explosively dangerous. Recent examples include Ebola, avian influenza, AIDS, and SARS. So whose fault is the spread of a virus like COVID-19? There is no doubt that it is spread from person to person. This may frequently be inadvertent. However, in cases where people consciously flouted government stipulations of social distancing or lockdown, then those who did so may have the death of others on their hands. What about crossover from the

---

[2] Donald A. Henderson (30 December 2011) "The eradication of smallpox – An overview of the past, present, and future", Vaccine, Vol. 29, D8. doi:10.1016/j.vaccine.2011.06.080. PMID 22188929.

[3] Laura Spinney, *Pale Rider: The Spanish Flu of 1918 and How It Changed the World* (London: Jonathan Cape, 2017), p. 352.

[4] Public Health England, *Surveillance of influenza and other respiratory viruses in the United Kingdom winter 2014 to 2015*, GOV.UK: http://www.gov.uk/phe (last viewed 8 April 2020).

animal to the human population in the first place? All the cases mentioned above came from people eating, or coming into close contact with, wild animals, including fruit bats and chimpanzees. So on neither count is the outbreak and spread of COVID-19 a "natural disaster". It could have been avoided. We have helped bring this about by forcing wild animals into closer proximity to humans, by consumption of bushmeat and by animal trafficking – often in defiance of local laws. In some Chinese markets, different live animal species were kept in close proximity, thus enabling the virus to move across species. The COVID-19 RNA is very similar to a coronavirus found in bats, and there is evidence that it may have been transmitted to humans via eating, or exposure to another animal, possibly a pangolin.

## Human reactions to infectious disease

Our reactions to pandemic diseases are diverse, varying personally, psychologically, culturally, and religiously. These factors include the following.

### Fear

Fear is a frequent and almost intuitive response to a life-threatening disease like COVID-19. There are several examples of this in the Bible. In the book of Job, the "friends" insist that Job must have sinned to have been stricken so devastatingly. Why would they be so insistent? Partly, because that was the orthodox cultural perspective on sickness and loss at the time, although such views persist even today in some religious communities. However, behind the orthodoxy was the real fear that if someone as righteous as Job could be so devastated by traumatic loss and disease, then that could happen to anyone – and that was scary! In 2 Kings 20 we read about King Hezekiah's fear from being told that he would become sick and die. His first, not last, resort was to turn his face to the wall, and then to pray. That is an example we could all copy.

## Panic

Fear of the disease may create panic over what actions are necessary for preserving health and life. The COVID-19 pandemic has spawned examples of this, such as panic buying and stockpiling of goods, actions that left supermarket shelves empty and certain sections of society unable to access even basic commodities. In Acts 27, we learn of terrified sailors in blind panic threatening to secretly abandon their ship during a fierce storm, leaving the Apostle Paul and other passengers to die if the ship was overwhelmed. Paul's response of prayer and confidence in God saved the day and the lives of all concerned.

## Corruption

It is commonly said that disasters bring out the best and the worst in human beings. There can be a very dark side to disasters. Sadly, the COVID-19 threat exposed this aspect of life vividly in various forms of corruption that arose. It seems as if scammers regard a pandemic as open season, preying on the vulnerable in society. Most damaging of all are the schemes that a few commercial businesses, and even some corrupt politicians, employed to ensure they could benefit financially from the threats the disease posed. COVID-19 requires all of us to rethink the socio-economic systems and structures we have lived under in the post-war era. In particular, the pandemic, though global in nature, has exposed the social and economic inequities that low-income countries suffer under the dominant forms of global capitalism, thereby making them even more vulnerable to the virus.

## Blame and denial

Because society finds it convenient to lay the blame for a pandemic on something, or someone, there is a corresponding urge to also deny responsibility. One of the lasting socio-political and economic legacies that our responses to pandemics can leave is the breakdown of social cohesion due to allegations that colour, ethnicity, or nationality are responsible for the pandemic. Perhaps the most common allegation during the COVID-19 pandemic was the labelling of it as the "Chinese virus", because the city of Wuhan, in China, was where it first erupted. Once the virus spread to other countries, instances of Chinese citizens being insulted or assaulted were reported. One president insisted on naming it the "China virus", because it came from China, he explained. On the other hand, because the authorities in Wuhan, and perhaps within the Chinese national party too, initially denied that there was a problem, addressing the spread of the virus was delayed, which allowed a pandemic to develop. Labels, justified or not, have a habit of spreading blame and denial.

Another form of denial, which is distinctly religious, comes from theologies that either deny the existence of disease, or which guarantee protection or healing for those who have sufficient faith. Although we fully recognize the reality of direct divine healing, we can see no Christian theological basis for guarantees of immunity, for denial of clinically recognized diseases, or for distrust of healing through medicine. We also place under this category of blame and denial the conspiracy theories concerning the origins of this virus, which have abounded during the COVID-19 pandemic.

## Passivity

Types of denial can be personal. Some fear facing up to reality, others fear that there is little or nothing one can do to change anything because the disease is rampant. The first type involves denying the reality of the seriousness of the disease, and refusing to abide by mitigation measures, such as social distancing, isolation, quarantine, etc. It may involve seeking the company of like-minded peer groups who depend upon their close social contacts to maintain the group denial, while defying officialdom's restriction of their association and movements. The second type involves facing up to the reality of the disease but becoming paralyzed by the enormity of it all. Seeing little point in implementing mitigation measures, there is submission with an inert passivity to "the will of God". There are parallels here to responses to climate change, which is arguably a far greater long-term threat than COVID-19. The threats posed by pandemics have long been recognized, but little was done in most countries to prepare for them: likewise the dangers of climate change have been extensively documented for many years, not least by the Intergovernmental Panel on Climate Change, but there is little evidence of a serious international response to the threats posed by climate change.

## Altruism and compassion

Last but by no means least, either in quality or in quantity, extreme disease catastrophes often prompt signature acts of altruism, as the COVID-19 pandemic has also demonstrated. Among the general populations of affected countries around the world, altruistic compassion has been one of the most positive and encouraging responses that has emerged from the crisis. Whether taking proactive care of the elderly and vulnerable in communities, risking infection to deliver vital supplies and food, or coming out of retirement to care for the sick, many people have responded to the evident needs with a selfless desire to alleviate the suffering of those around them.

## Theology and science

In our modern, highly interconnected world, pandemics are one of the most frightening dangers facing humanity. They can travel at the speed of a jet airliner, yet viruses cannot be seen. Humanity's best protection against a new virus such as COVID-19 remains the very basic and long-understood method of isolating infected people from others. If we don't know who is infected, then we simply have to keep everyone apart as far as possible. This has become known as "social distancing" and self-isolation. In the case of COVID-19, it shut down large parts of the economy and of normal life in countries around the world. The only available medical intervention was to keep people alive as long as possible by treating the symptoms while allowing the body time to develop its own immunity.

A striking example of self-sacrifice in the face of a pandemic is the case of the villagers of Eyam in northern England when bubonic plague (the "Black Death") reached it from London in late summer 1665. Though they didn't know the cause of the plague and had no treatment or cure for it, under the leadership of Revd William Mompesson the entire village of 800 people decided to isolate themselves to prevent its onward transmission in the area. As a result of this self-sacrifice, led by the church, one third of the population died, including the vicar's wife. But the surrounding area was spared the plague.

Christians have long seen care for the sick and the dying as a primary duty. Monasteries and hospices have provided succour and care since the early centuries of the church.[5] Medical missions have often been, and remain, the focus of the overseas work of many Christian bodies and aid agencies.

One of the remarkable, but often unconsidered, aspects of the universe is that it is an ordered, consistent place. An understanding of the orderliness of nature, which was fostered by the Protestant Reformation and the Enlightenment in the sixteenth and seventeenth centuries, allowed science and technology to develop to their position of strength today. Many of the founders of the Royal Society of London, whose origin in 1660 marks the point at which science as we know it really became organized, were Christians who wanted to use their scientific studies for the good of humankind.[6] Medical advances that save lives are one outcome of scientific endeavours. Strong messages from faith leaders of

[5] Amanda Porterfield, *Healing in the History of Christianity* (Oxford, UK: Oxford University Press, 2009), p. 230.

[6] Peter Harrison (2006), "The Bible and the emergence of modern science", Science & Christian Belief, Vol. 18, pp. 115–32. Also R. S. White, "Take ten: Scientists and their religious beliefs", in Stephen Finamore and John Weaver (ed.), *Wisdom, Science and the Scriptures* (Oxford, UK: Regents Park College, 2012), pp. 157–79.

the importance of collaboration between science and faith are a powerful source of education and changed behaviour. We fear that lives are lost for want of such collaborations. For instance, in tackling the recent Ebola epidemics in West and central Africa, Linda Mobula and others have told us that it eventually required a collaboration between scientists and local community religious adherents to bring about the eradication of this terrible disease in the areas where it was killing so many.[7]

A striking aspect of the COVID-19 pandemic is the speed and extent with which scientific understanding has been shared. The genome sequence was shared *internationally* by Chinese scientists within weeks of the first outbreak there. This allowed work to commence immediately and without delay in laboratories around the world on developing vaccines, antiviral drugs, tests for the presence of the virus, and antibody tests: these developments are what ultimately breaks the power of a virus and allows normal life to recommence.

From a Christian perspective, it is an indication of God's goodness to us that he has created a fruitful, comprehensible world in which we can use our scientific understanding of physical and medical processes for the good of humankind. Then we can use that knowledge to put precautions in place to limit the damage, reduce the vulnerability, and increase the resilience of people at risk, and to mitigate or change our behaviours so as to reduce the likelihood of future disasters such as pandemics.

Christians see the reality of the brokenness of this world, but also the truth of God's sovereignty over it and of his ultimate plans for a new creation. That does not mean that we need not strive to improve things now. Rather, it points in the opposite direction: that we should work for better scientific and medical understanding of pandemics; that we should enable communities to build resilience against them; and that we should strive to remove the unjust disparities in wealth and resources that

---

[7] See Chapter 4 by Linda Mobula.

mean it is often the poor, the sick, and the elderly who are most vulnerable and who suffer most. Jesus would surely want us to use our understanding of his creation for the good of others. The sense of lament that we may be driven to by seeing the impact of disasters such as the COVID-19 pandemic is a right and proper response of Christians; while spurring us on to continue working and struggling to bring justice and reconciliation in this world, we should long for the return of Christ and the inauguration of the new creation (Romans 8:18–22).

## Pastoral responses

The passage of Scripture in Philippians 2:1–9 encapsulates the response Christians should have toward each other and toward their neighbours, and it is especially relevant at a time of pandemic. Out of selfless deference, as modelled by the Godhead in the incarnation (Philippians 2:6–9), the Apostle Paul in this passage provides many practical comments regarding response to a pandemic.

### The witness of Christians selflessly serving the interests of others

Such service, both in the church and wider communities, is a far more effective demonstration of Christian faith than an appeal to a philosophical theodicy. Jesus said that it will be by their fruits that Christians shall be known more than by apologetic arguments; in other words, the most powerful apologetic for a time such as a pandemic is living out the words of Paul in his letter to the Philippians. In the third century, Bishop Cyprian, after whom was named a famous plague epidemic which struck across the Roman empire, urged Christians to care for the living while remaining among them. Similarly, Martin Luther in the sixteenth century remained in Wittenberg, to care for the sick and dying, rather than fleeing. Because of self-denying actions by Christians in the face of such epidemics, history shows that there was often subsequent widespread growth in the churches. In the context of a pandemic, it is also the case that self-denying actions such as social distancing may also serve the best interests of others; this is especially so with COVID-19 because the infection may be spread for several days before a person knows that they have the disease.

## Providing pastoral support and care for health-workers and their families

Often health-workers are wrestling with the tensions of going to work. They are helping the sick and dying, with accompanying risks to their own health, while their own families may wish they could stay at home. Balancing these commitments and loyalties can be a huge emotional and spiritual strain on health-workers and their families, and church communities need to come together to ensure that they are diligent and effective in helping to support the needs of those on the front line, both during and after this pandemic.

## Encouraging conversations about death and dying

Everyone should be doing this anyway, since death is the most certain outcome of life for everyone. A time of pandemic can make the point of such conversations more urgent and more relevant. However, the Apostle Paul's words and the model to which he appeals sharpen the focus toward even laying down one's life for the sake of others. In the case of pandemics, where the disease is rampant, where both staff and patients may die, and where medical resources may become overwhelmed, such focused conversations are necessary. As one hospital chaplain told us, "People need to start thinking about their possible death: do they want to go to hospital? Do they want a ventilator?" Such conversations may not be easy, but Christians need never be fearful and hopeless, as the Paul's earlier words make clear, "For to me to live is Christ, and to die is gain" (Philippians 1:21, ESV). Discussions about death should surely be among the most common conversations within the Christian community, because, as Paul says later in his letter to the Philippians, "our citizenship is in heaven, and from it we await a Savior, the Lord Jesus Christ, who will transform our lowly body to be like his glorious body" (Philippians 3:20–21). Bishop Cyprian made the same point in a famous sermon which is still preserved: "if you truly believe [in God], why do you, who are destined to be with Christ and secure in the promise of the Lord, not rejoice that you are called to Christ and be glad that you are free from the devil?"[8]

## Providing robust theological and pastoral care for the sick, dying, and the bereaved

This should be the kind of sensitive, discerning care that is helpful, where, in the words of one Christian scholar, "words we would not utter to ease another's grief we ought not to speak to satisfy our own sense of piety".[9] This is of particular importance when many patients die alone, with relatives unable to visit because of concerns about spreading the virus. It will also not only be the remit of church leaders and professional clergy to offer such care, but the scale of this pandemic means that every Christian must be ready to listen intently to those who are in the midst of suffering and to offer the comfort of Christ, and the promise of hope in the new creation where they can.

## Re-evaluating life's values and purpose

COVID-19 has turned our worlds upside-down in many ways. Disasters such as this pandemic may also encourage people to re-evaluate what is important in life, which sometimes turns them

---

[8] Cyprian, *De Mortalitate*, available in modern English translation from http://www.ntslibrary.com/PDF%20Books/MORTALITY%20by%20 St%20Cyprian.pdf (last viewed 8 April 2020).

[9] David B. Hart, *The Doors of the Sea: Where Was God in the Tsunami?* (Grand Rapids, MI: Eerdmans, 2011), p. 99.

to reliance on God; to examine themselves as to what, in the light this disease shines upon us, is worthwhile in their life, and what is actually worthless (2 Corinthians 5:10). As C. S. Lewis wrote: "God whispers to us in our pleasures, speaks in our conscience, but shouts in our pains: it is His megaphone to rouse a deaf world".[10]

Although COVID-19 is a disease that has forced separation and isolation from others, ironically it has made us appreciate the value of community relationships, of reaching out to friends and neighbours, of realizing the theological truth that "the reason for my life is yours", whoever you are (Philippians 2:4; Luke 10:25–37). It is a common testimony among survivors that in the wake of shared disasters such as COVID-19 they found a sense of belonging, of growing together, and of sharing and coping with deep emotions and experiences that were absent in normal life.

Christians do not view the fear and struggles with life that are so apparent in the midst of a pandemic to be the chief focus of their stories; they don't just seek an end to the pandemic. The end to which Christians look forward is that which is promised by God to them when Jesus returns, that is, the promise of a new heaven and a new earth, where righteousness dwells (2 Peter 3:13). In that new creation there will be no more sickness or death, and thus "neither shall there be mourning, nor crying, nor pain anymore, for the former things [will] have passed away" (Revelation 21:4, ESV). This is the heart of the gospel, the good news of Jesus Christ.

## Offering a preferential option for the poor, the weak, and the neglected

The COVID-19 virus is no respecter of persons; it is affecting royalty; prime ministers; white-collar, factory, and shop workers alike. However, access to appropriate treatment may be more exclusive. On a global scale, those who can afford it will likely

---

[10] Lewis, *The Problem of Pain,* p. 74.

be able to access superior and speedier access to healthcare than those who are poor. The majority of the latter live in more cramped conditions where water, sanitation, hygiene, and medical infrastructure is broken, thus facilitating the lethal spread of the disease more rapidly. Elderly people are also more vulnerable and are often isolated. These inequities in our world implicate every one of us. Christian churches should develop strategies for self-giving care for the weakest in their fellowships and wider communities, both at home and abroad.

Of course, a big challenge to the church will be what to do once the world begins to return to "normal". It would surely be a huge missed opportunity if our Christian perspectives and practices were not to adapt and change in the wake of such a truly worldwide event. The raised visibility of the vulnerable among us and the refocus of our media gaze from vacuous celebrity to those who actually keep our societies going is a chance for all of us to reassess the culture we have helped create. The church, as followers of Christ, should be at the forefront of making sure that conversations are steered toward justice and mercy for the whole of God's creation.

A man who shouted across the car park to one of us, as he came out of a doctor's surgery at the time of the COVID-19 crisis, couldn't have stated it better: "We surely need God to help us now, don't we?"

# AFTERWORD

## ROGER ABBOTT AND ROBERT WHITE

Ending a book of this kind is not an easy task for editors. We are extremely thankful to each author who has contributed to this project, for taking the time, in addition to speaking at the workshop, to contribute a chapter to this book. As editors, we did not impose any restrictions on what they had to write, other than addressing the same theme they presented on at the workshop in April 2018, and, of course, adhering to a general word limit. As indicated in the introduction, we chose keynote speakers for the workshop from among academics, responder–practitioners, and survivors of major disasters to ensure we covered as many aspects of disasters, faith, and resilience as were feasible. We believe this book reflects this same range. Of course, authors take final responsibility for their own chapters.

Diverse in their skills though they were, and with an even more diverse body of participants, it was clear during the workshop that from whichever category speakers and participants came, they each held one another in great respect, with no one being regarded as superior or inferior to anyone else. That is not to say that we all agreed about everything; we did not, and that is not a bad thing, allowing for further critical thinking from us all. However, it is true to say that what we may have disagreed upon paled into insignificance when compared with the amount we did agree on. Furthermore, given that most of us would not have ever met, or even known of, many of the others before we came together at the workshop, this level of agreement can only be a good thing as well. We trust that the same kind of mutual humility and respect between authors has been discerned while reading the book to this point, and that this final chapter will not damage that important image! This relative unity is not an insignificant point to mention because, frankly, humility and mutual respect have not been the most striking features to grace the realm of modern disaster response, generally speaking.

## The perils of hubris

Several rather negative factors responsible for a widespread lack of humility come to mind. For instance, in the disaster response world, a feature that has all too often bedevilled this particular area has been what are dubbed as "turf wars". Disaster response is, inevitably, a multi-agency, and often an international, phenomenon. It frequently involves huge numbers of different agencies and large numbers of statutory, professional, and volunteer staff, involving many faiths and none. The response to the Lockerbie bombing, to Hurricane Katrina, to the Haiti earthquake, and to the supertyphoon in the Philippines, mentioned in the previous chapters, each demonstrates the point. Each event has also demonstrated the problem of "turf-wars" as well. That is, where particular agents/-cies have developed and corralled their field of expertise so tenaciously that they have refused, or simply not thought to give time and space, to listening to, sharing with, and learning from the experiences and expertise of other fields. Our (White and Abbott's) chapter on the COVID-19 pandemic draws attention to the contribution to the spread of the virus that the Wuhan authorities made when they did not initially give a full picture of the severity of the epidemic in their city. This is another aspect of hubris that is too common in disasters. One aspect of this neglect we are currently interested in from our research at The Faraday Institute, into so-called natural disasters, is the neglect by geoscientists and theologians to collaborate: maybe by design or perhaps more commonly unthinkingly so.

In fact, the partnership that has been working at The Faraday Institute since 2012 between White, a geophysicist, and Abbott, a practical theologian, is one that challenges the "conflict thesis" that still underlies so much of the science–faith discussion.

The thesis is that science and religion are, by definition and practice, necessarily in conflict. Our conviction is that, in the realm of disasters, resolving this conflict can save many lives and livelihoods. However, a singularly dangerous consequence of the conflict thesis has been a claim to owning territory that, in their view, each party feels the other one must not be able to claim or trespass upon. Furthermore, in reality, it has also meant that with respect to disaster prevention research and practice there has not been the collaboration, either at the levels of academic research or in professional or volunteer practice, that there could be, and should be if lives and livelihoods are to be saved and injuries spared. We believe that such "turf wars" may contribute to lives and livelihoods lost; in theological terms, "turf wars" contribute to evil and not to reducing it (Galatians 5:15).

Of course, as this book has shown, every particular event or disaster is unique, both in terms of the physical nature of it and of the impact it has upon our personal, emotional, and material lives. Even gender brings its unique consequences to a disaster as the contribution from Marie and Lucie shows: it provides some insight into the personal struggles that disasters present for women, who, research informs us, tend to become more clinically traumatized than men. The fact that this mother and daughter were spared such depth of trauma is due, they and we both believe, to the value of their Christian faith. Earthquakes affect people differently to floods; disease has its own particular impacts, as does a terrorist attack in mid-air. However, every disaster is, potentially, a rich learning opportunity for facing the next one, for academics, for responder–practitioners, and for survivors. Yet, having been involved in responding to disasters at both responder–practitioner and academic levels since the 1980s, we could make the point, as we did at a gathering of local authority emergency planners and responders in Cornwall just a few years ago, that what strikes us now is how little we have learned, at least when it comes to the human aspects. Following each disaster, multiple research projects ensue and volumes of literature are published, including the inevitable "Official

Reports and Recommendations". What is astonishing is just how much repetition of the same lessons needing to be learned is found in successive reports! This is the case all too often, we find, with disasters at home or abroad, involving national and local governments or national (NGO) or international non-governmental organizations (INGO).

Added to the professional "turf war" hubris and needless repetition is also the abhorrent profit motive that is endemic in the disaster response industry today. As with the rampant neoliberal free-market capitalism that governs so much of the modern economic world, so it is with the economics of disaster capitalism (for further reading, see Naomi Klein, *The Shock Doctrine,* and Anthony Loewenstien, *Disaster Capitalism: Making a Killing out of Catastrophe*). The disaster relief industry is dangerously competitive in winning contracts and gaining donations, with huge sums of money at stake, an aspect that few can claim immunity from, even in the most stringently safeguarded INGOs. We await with interest to see what examples of commercial and political exploitation will emerge from the COVID-19 pandemic as time goes on.

Perhaps, though, the most grievous hubris of contemporary disaster response has been the way academics and response/ aid agencies in high-income countries have brought with them to low-income countries – where most catastrophic disasters happen to occur – their models, self-assuredly imposing them upon other countries and cultures. Our own research at The Faraday Institute, not least from the testimony of many survivors we have interviewed, bears witness to this trend as a source of deep regret, and of anger, on the part of those who are subject to these models. Perhaps none more so than the population of Haiti, as the chapters from Marie and Lucie, and Honorat indicate. In so many ways, we feel the 2010 Haiti earthquake has proven – dare we say it – a hopeful watershed in the field of disaster response? At last, we now discern an increasing voice coming out of faith-based organization policy-making at least, confirming the importance of INGOs first needing to respect, then learn from, local wisdom and knowledge before they implement anything. Asking, listening, and learning is taking the place of "we already know what is best for you, and this is what you need". Honorat, and Mobula also, have made reference to this point in their respective chapters. Whether it is for tackling the explosive Ebola disease in the Democratic Republic of the Congo – where Mobula discusses the sensitivity of inter-tribal cultural attitudes to sickness, to Western medicine, to religion, and to cooperative relations with each other – or whether it is in Haiti – where the "Republic of the NGOs" has reigned for far too long with too little to show for it in terms of progress and healing for that nation – the lesson is the same: stop, ask, listen, and learn. Earn the right to speak, let alone to practise in a disaster-stricken country. A similar sensitivity is required in tackling the COVID-19 virus in low-income countries globally. And then, when we go, we go with the attitude of being a guest, not a host, and certainly not as an occupier. We are there to give, not to take; to help, not to "milk".

Speaking of Western (all too often, but not exclusively, white) hubris in disaster management and response, we feel constrained by Mosey's chapter to raise the issue of political ownership, even sequestration, of disasters. This was also a key feature we found from our research in New Orleans, in Haiti, and in the Philippines – on top of the suffering and grief from the experiences of a natural hazard came the experiences from the "dark arts" of political shenanigans. There are distinct signs of this happening over the COVID-19 pandemic as well. Mosey's account of how the search for justice for their daughter, Helga, has been continually stymied at the highest levels of national and international political leadership is deeply disturbing. It does nothing to disarm the suspicions of there being some kind of political cover-up, lest some more disturbing elements of truth and injustice should come to light by a more open disclosure of the facts. The persistent disingenuousness and even silence of political and security institutions in massaging or silencing truth is a moral outrage which compassionate people need to bring pressure upon to end. In the dark sides of politics and militarism, now integrally involved in disasters (again see Loewenstien, *Disaster Capitalism*), it seems that transparency and accountability are awkward to live with, though, Mosey indicates, they are what the bereaved and survivors may want most, to help them adapt to the new normal they have to live with.

Too often in the wake of disasters, the fears of financial loss and blame are in league with each other. This leads to another form of hubris, by disaster lawyers and insurers this time. Disasters can lead to the dread of litigation by potentially culpable parties, and of massive claims on insurance companies. Neither of these is good for business or for companies' shares. On the other hand, disasters are a lawyer's and an insurer's "open season", as was seen to be the case in the aftermath of the flooding of New Orleans after Hurricane Katrina in 2005. Truth became a hostage to litigation and/or to fears of financial losses through payments of compensation and prolonged battles over insurance claims. All too often this perpetuates the myth that drives the disaster litigation industry, that what the "victims" want most is compensation measured in monetary terms. As if all the money in the world can compensate for someone, or some place, you have loved, and feel you are dying every day to see again. All too often this myth silences the truth that what "victims" actually want most is the truth about what happened and how it happened, and the assurance that as much will be done as is possible to ensure that it cannot happen again. Broken hearts can never be healed by money, but they can find an aid to healing through truth. We shudder to think what litigious outcomes may emerge from the COVID-19 pandemic once the "lockdowns" are over and the true impact on businesses and employment become apparent. Will societies be as willing to engage together in recovering from the financial losses from the pandemic as they were for engaging with the "lockdowns" to save lives? The jury is out.

A substantial injection of humility and transparency could save lives, health, and even profits, in the arena of disaster management and response. We have seen too many commercial and political businesses get their comeuppance following a refusal to tell the truth. The immediate aftermath of Hurricane Katrina saw that happen in the city, state, and federal government, and possibly the same fate awaits certain politicians and business persons connected with Haiti. Human nature still thinks it can deride the divine warning, "Do not be deceived: God is not mocked, for whatever one sows, that will he also reap" (Galatians 6:7, ESV).

## The common grace of humanitarianism

Moving on from the above more negative lessons, what has also come across very powerfully and positively in the book has been the enormous demonstrations of humanitarianism that disasters reveal. Each of our survivors has written about this fact. Mosey spoke of the huge support he and his wife and son experienced from their church members and from correspondents. Honorat saw it happen soon after the Haiti earthquake with the arrival of the US Marines bringing them supplies of food and medicine just when they needed it most. Marie and Lucie received material assistance provided by NGOs and INGOs, as well as by diaspora family members in the USA while they were living in the IDP camp. Taylor spoke of it in terms of the Arkansas Baptist Convention's Baptist Builders' arrival in flooded New Orleans, in the vast numbers of volunteers from all over the USA who came to the rescue of New Orleanians, and in the coming together of the Gentilly residents as they gradually returned home, while their state and federal governments failed them so miserably. We (White and Abbott) have drawn attention to altruism being a recurrent feature of the response to the COVID-19 pandemic. Not least has been the global commitment of front-line healthcare staff to working in areas of high risk to their own lives in their bid to save the lives of the sick.

As Abbott commented, too often we can memorialize the suffering and the evils of a disaster, and forget just how much good the same event can display. Frequently a disaster can totally transform normally privatized, soulless urban populations into communities of enormous and astounding friendliness, kindness, and generosity. This personal reflection by a Katrina survivor, on display in the New Orleans Museum of Arts as part of a 10th anniversary Katrina exhibition, is a case in point: "I remember after Katrina meeting one of my neighbors who at the time we thought was 'the mean old lady in the neighbourhood.' When we saw each other after the storm it was like our friendship started at that moment because we realized how petty the arguments were". If transformations like this were not the case in the particular disasters mentioned in this book, then how much more dreadful would these disasters have become? Rebecca Solnit has done us a great service in highlighting this fact with specific vignettes contained in her book *Paradise in Hell* (chapter 3). Abbott also set out a theological basis for this phenomenon in his chapter on the goodness of God, where he commented on the common good that is so often, and so remarkably, an aspect of even the most appalling of disasters (see also Abbott, *Sit on Our Hands or Stand on Our Feet*, pp. 181–93). So remarkable is it that the phenomenon compels some accountability equal to, if not greater than, the more dominant focus of attention that is given to the aspects of evil. From the Christian theological perspective, we account for this overflow of good in terms of the doctrine of God's common grace. This God, as Moo has reminded us, is the God who "makes his sun rise on the evil and on the good, and sends rain on the just and on the unjust" (Matthew 5:45, ESV). He is the God whose loudest response to the challenge from suffering and evil is not some philosophical theodicy (something that no one has ever yet been able to provide satisfactorily in all the centuries of scholars trying to do so). Rather, God's response is a practical theodicy of his demonstrable goodness and grace that is capable of descending onto a catastrophe and suffocating the oxygen of evil. Just as when God descended into this world of suffering and pain, taking on flesh and blood and a human soul, to be "God with us" in the person of Jesus Christ. Then, even those who could not fathom who he really was had to confess that he was "good" (Luke 18:18). Ironically, it was the sufferings and death of Christ – where evil acted most perniciously – that proved the ultimate triumph of good over evil, by virtue of Christ's resurrection from the dead and the assured, ultimate conquest of evil (John 19:30; Acts 2:22–24; 1 Corinthians 15:54–57; Revelation 20:4–21:6).

## Our Christian perspective

Perhaps this is an appropriate place to state clearly something that readers may have noticed already. This is a book that unashamedly considers disasters from an overtly Christian perspective. In fact, this same particularist perspective caught a few unawares and was commented upon by our workshop participants at the time. Our defence for this focus, if such is needed, is twofold. First, The Faraday Institute for Science and Religion is a research institute that holds a "Christian ethos" to be a fundamental tenet of its existence. This by no means suggests that there is any less of a scholarly or practical regard held for other religions, or for other ways of meaning. Nor does it suggest that other religions or ways of meaning are held in lesser respect.

Anyone who has had to study and/or work in disasters will know that disasters do not show favours to different religions or religious communities. As Christians, we recognize fully that disasters cause death and suffering to people of all faiths and none. Christian responder–practitioners to disasters have to be prepared to work in full collaboration with survivors and responder–practitioners of other faiths and with those of no faith, and have to respond in different cultures than their own. Mobula has to do this wherever she is deployed as a disaster-response medic. Mosey has served as advisor to statutory authorities and response agencies. Abbott has to do this in his role as responder–practitioner too, and he has written a theological justification for such collaborations of mutual respect and friendship, rooted in God's common grace theology (Abbott, *Sit on Our Hands or Stand on Our Feet*, pp. 309–60). Indeed, we would be disappointed by Christians who felt it wrong to respond to disasters by resisting such collaborations in the name of defending their faith. It is our considered view that interfaith *friendship* need not involve particular faith compromise.

A second point to our rationale for a Christian perspective lies in our academic hesitation to align with the common sociological perspective where religion is often considered as a generic concept.[1] We believe that this perspective is a product of modern secularism and is disingenuous and, potentially, disrespectful to the particularisms of the different religions. Having conducted research in disaster zones involving different religions and religious denominations, we feel that an approach that carries most integrity is a particularist one. This is the one we chose to adopt for the workshop and for this book.

## Un-natural disasters

As a Christian, who is also a geophysicist, White has presented us with an overview of the relationship that exists between the different kinds of natural hazard that are an essential aspect of the goodness of God's creation of the natural world, and of how important they are to the sustenance of the most beautiful planet in the universe, planet Earth, which we inhabit. White's geoscientific (as well as theological) perspective on natural hazards and how they can turn into disasters, chimes well with the opening theological chapter that Moo provided for us. Both authors emphasize the persistent goodness of creation (yet another feature of the divine attribute Abbott focuses upon in more strictly theological and narrative terms). Both also suggest strongly that natural hazards turn into disasters more often than not because of human attitudes and interventions that run counter

---

[1] E. P. O'Connell, R. P. Abbott, R. S. White (2019) "'Generic' versus 'mature' measures of Christian religiosity: Comparing two quantitative measures of religiosity", European Journal of Mental Health, Vol. 14, Iss. 1, pp. 21–40. https://doi.org/10.5708/EJMH.14.2019.1.2

to the Creator's wisdom and will. In so doing, Moo and White add a strong theological, geophysical, and environmental case to the argument many social and physical geographers have been making for dropping the word "natural" from describing disasters. Retention of that term runs the risk of deflecting attention away from the very human individual, and the structural, social, and political injustices and inequities that are frequently the real cause for a natural hazard turning into a disaster.

One of the most obvious, and one of the most serious, examples of human causation in disasters involving natural hazards must be that of climate change, as White touched on and Rollinson has more concertedly drawn to our attention (see also Bell and White, *Creation Care and the Gospel*; Moo and White, *Hope in an Age of Despair*). We (White and Abbott) aver that in the case of pandemics, it is increasingly apparent that human behaviours may well be largely responsible for the viral transmission from wild animals to humans, and from humans to humans. Yet, even with regards to this issue, there are still those who will not accept that humans are the main agents at fault – they also deny that there is any real crisis involved. Here, once again, we hit resistance when it comes to the legitimate, and essential, role that the science should be permitted to play. It is our view that this role for the science can also be played out in collaboration with Christian theology and practice without any compromise to either discipline. Rollinson's reminder to us about the divine mandate we have all received to manage the creation as agents of God is one we all have to take seriously, and one for which we shall all have to give account to God one day. This responsibility is an aspect of our doing good as those who are created in the image of a good God (Genesis 1:27, 31). A key part to that stewardship must surely be to have regard to the science, and to its rightful application. Rollinson stresses that for low-income country populations, climate change is already at such a level that it is influencing the severity and rate of occurrence of natural hazards that are already turning disastrous. Therefore, in addressing climate change with the urgency it warrants, there is a mitigative action each one of us can take in our personal and community daily living as well as on national and international levels. Without this urgency, the risk of natural hazards turning disastrous – especially, but never exclusively, for those in low-income countries – will only increase in spite of all the human good will and vast financial aid that will still pour in for emergency responses.

## The value of Christian faith

As we come to the close of this afterword, we now reflect upon what has been a recurring theme running throughout the book, just as it ran through the keynote presentations of the workshop, namely: the significant value of the Christian faith in disaster response. This is not an exclusive claim over the merits of other faiths. It is simply a conclusion from the particular perspective this book offers, and also from the research on the subject we have carried out at The Faraday Institute. The narrative contributions of each of the survivor authors (Mosey, Marie, Lucie, Honorat, and Taylor) have testified to the great value they, and others, gained from their Christian faith when faced with catastrophic circumstances. In each case, they found it was their faith in God through Jesus Christ that brought them through. Contrary to the common media perception that such terrible events must surely destroy any serious thinking person's trust in a God who is good, they found the complete opposite to be true. This observation resonates closely with the research findings from our research projects on exploring how religious beliefs (principally Christian, it so happens) influenced the way that survivors of catastrophic disasters involving natural hazards responded to and recovered from those events. Of the hundreds of survivors we have interviewed in the course of our research, less than a handful spoke of any doubting their faith, let alone of any rejection of it. Of course, the Christian faith allows for doubting, as the disciple of Jesus, Thomas, reminds us. Lament too is another resource granted to the traumatized survivor of catastrophe, where survivors can pour out their anger, confusion, and fear to God in Job-like fashion. Christianity does not endorse a stoical attitude for disaster survivors. Nearly two-thirds of the book of the Psalms, in the Bible, is made up of such laments. However, these operate on a completely different level from hurt attitudes that reject the faith altogether. Lamenting to God is different from lamenting against God.

A further finding we have found in our research, however, is less encouraging when it comes to the value of the Christian faith, as we have found it being applied in disaster contexts. We refer to the fact that our research shows that although the faith of our participant survivors did serve to comfort them in their trauma by providing a framework of meaning for what they went through, it did not, in many cases, direct them as to how they might mitigate future encounters with natural hazards. One of the reasons why this did not happen was because there was no real connection between the science that could provide so much education and knowledge in how to adapt to and to adjust one's life to living safely with natural hazards, and their theology and faith (for further expansion on this point, see Abbott and White, *Narratives of Faith from the Haiti Earthquake*). It was a similar disconnect that Mobula found with her work with local tribal groups in West, and central, Africa and their suspicions of Western doctors helping treat the Ebola epidemics. Here is another area where Christian communities need to discover ways they can make the connection and collaborate with science in the interests of saving lives and livelihoods. The will to collaborate is necessary from both parties, and mutual respect, humility, and sensitivity is essential to the process.

We hope that the chapters in this book, inclusive of our research involving both geoscience and theology, will serve as contributions toward furthering rejection, not just of the aforementioned conflict thesis between science and religion, but also of the increasingly weakening secular thesis. This thesis states that religion will most surely become extinct in the face of the modernist secularization of societies. There are still too many remnants of that thesis alive within disaster management and response circles: thinking that relegates the value of religious beliefs to a bygone age, and which even sees religion as being responsible for causing more problems, through such attitudes of passivity as religious fatalism, rather than helping solve them. It is a thesis that, at best, may offer a paternalistic and patronizingly limited role to Christian church premises as emergency shelters and safe havens; it even may be willing to draw upon the huge Christian volunteer base for humanitarian services, with the strings attached that there is no mention of religion as such.

## Voices worth taking notice of

The narratives provided by survivors in this book, and collected in our research interviews, are by no means a statistically representative group. However, given the severity of the disaster incidents they encountered, they certainly warrant being taken seriously when it comes to the significance their religious beliefs and faith held for them. We therefore would recommend this book as an important contribution to the growing narrative, and in some instances, the empirical data, for including Christian communities into disaster planning, management, and response from both logistical and therapeutic service perspectives. From the same data, we recommend that Christian communities engage more seriously with the scientific communities for the mitigation of disasters. If this book can make such a contribution in both of these directions, then we feel confident that the wishes of those who took part in the workshop – namely, that what was presented and learned would not be "kicked into the long grass" or consigned to the archives of academic libraries – will have been fulfilled.

What Mosey found that day he read, in the Apostle Paul's letter to the Romans (12:21), "Do not be overcome by evil, but overcome evil with good", is surely as powerful a practical response to disasters as we need. We believe this book justifies that claim, and that the contributions and recommendations contained in it can demonstrate how practical and transformative a theodicy it can truly be.

# AUTHOR PROFILES

**Hugh Rollinson** is Course Director at The Faraday Institute and Emeritus Professor of Earth Sciences at the University of Derby. After graduating from Oxford, Hugh worked for a number of years as a field geologist in the Geological Survey of Sierra Leone. This was followed by a PhD at the University of Leicester and then a postdoc at the University of Leeds. He then joined the University of Gloucestershire and worked there for 20 years, during which time he took a three-year leave of absence to work as Associate Professor of Geology and Head of Department in the University of Zimbabwe. He then took a position as Professor of Earth Sciences and Department Head at Sultan Qaboos University in Oman for six years, after which he served as Professor of Earth Sciences and Department Head at the University of Derby. Hugh is a Fellow of the Geological Society, a Chartered Geologist, and a Senior Fellow of the Higher Education Academy. His publications include *Early Earth Systems*.

**John Mosey** is the father of Helga who was one of the 270 victims of the Lockerbie air disaster of 21 December 1988. He has been a Pentecostal Church pastor for many years and has a special interest in working with orphans in India and the Philippines. John has given hundreds of talks and seminars on grief, forgiveness, and Christianity in churches all over the world. He spent 16 years working for Disaster Action, helping victims' relatives and working with police, social services, and others involved in the aftermath of disasters including the Kings Cross fire, the sinking of the Herald of Free Enterprise ferry, and the Piper Alpha fire. His experience has been drawn upon by academics, politicians, and by policy formers.

**Jonathan Moo** is Lindaman Chair and Associate Professor of New Testament and Environmental Studies at Whitworth University in Spokane, Washington, where his teaching encompasses courses in New Testament, Greek, exegesis, science and faith, and environmental studies. Jonathan completed his PhD in the Divinity Faculty at the University of Cambridge and holds previous degrees in Biology, English, Ecology, and Biblical studies. He is also President of Friends of Faraday USA. He has written extensively on different areas of his academic and practical expertise.

**Ken Taylor** started out his working life in the legal profession before gaining further qualifications in librarianship and in pastoral ministry. He holds the Chester L. Quarles Chair of Urban Missions at the New Orleans Baptist Theological Seminary. He is also pastor of Gentilly Baptist Church, New Orleans. He possesses a wealth of personal experience of Hurricane Katrina (2005) and its catastrophic impact on the flooding of the seminary, upon his family and their home, upon his church, and upon the surrounding neighbourhood. He has a special interest in community-focused ministry by the local church. He has co-edited *Etiquette and Taboos around the World: A Geographic Encyclopedia of Social and Cultural Customs*, and has contributed prolifically to a number of encyclopedias.

**Linda Mobula** received her MD at the University of California, San Francisco, and did a residency at Johns Hopkins Bayview Medical Center, followed by a post-doctoral fellowship at Johns Hopkins Hospital. She is Assistant Professor at Johns Hopkins School of Medicine, and Associate Researcher at the Johns Hopkins Bloomberg School of Public Health. Her speciality is response to natural and human-caused disasters that occur around the world. She responded to the Ebola outbreaks in the Democratic Republic of the Congo and West Africa, to the earthquake in Haiti (2010), to the supertyphoon in the Philippines (2013), and to the Syrian refugee crisis in Lesbos, Greece.

**Luc Honorat** is a senior pastor based in the town of Grand-Goâve, Haiti, located some 30 miles (50 km) west of the capital, Port-au-Prince. He is pastor of a Christian complex accommodating a school, a children's home, and a large church. He also oversees a number of satellite churches in the western and northern departments of Haiti. Grand-Goâve experienced catastrophic damage to life and property from the 2010 earthquake that devastated the region. He has commanded huge respect in his community for his dedication to social justice and to community renewal. He has worked to build resilience in the face of earthquake risk and the area's vulnerability to routine storms and their impact on a fragile infrastructure.

**Marie and Lucie** are mother and daughter Haitian survivors of the catastrophic earthquake which struck the Caribbean country of Haiti in 2010. They lived in the capital, Port-au-Prince, and are committed Christians. Their familial bond, integrity, and courage are typical of many women of faith in Haiti. Their vulnerability as women illustrates the gender-based struggle many Haitian women face in ordinary life as well as during tragedy.

**Robert (Bob) White** is Professor of Geophysics in the Department of Earth Sciences at Cambridge University and Director of The Faraday Institute for Science and Religion. He was elected a Fellow of the Royal Society in 1994, and a Fellow of the American Geophysical Union in 2016. In 2018, he was awarded a Gold Medal of the Royal Astronomical Society, which is their highest award, in recognition of a lifetime's achievement in research. He is also a Fellow of the Geological Society, an elected Member of the International Society for Science and Religion, and several other professional bodies. His publications include *Narratives of Faith from the Haiti Earthquake, Who is to Blame? Nature, Disasters, and Acts of God*, and *Hope in an Age of*

*Despair: The Gospel and the Future of Life on Earth*. He has also published extensively in numerous scientific journals.

**Roger Abbott** is Senior Research Associate in "Natural" Disasters for The Faraday Institute, Cambridge. Following many years in pastoral work, where his first introductions to responding to disasters were learned, he went on to gain his PhD in a practical theology of major incident response in the UK, before expanding his research experience more globally with The Faraday Institute. His publications include *Sit on Our Hands, or Stand on Our Feet?*, *Hello? Is Anyone There?*, and *Narratives of Faith from the Haiti Earthquake*. He has published in journals such as *Religions* and *Practical Theology*. He has also been a volunteer chaplain responder to major disasters in the UK and abroad.

Readers are invited to go to faraday.institute/Disasters or scan the code, where they can access videos of authors being interviewed, and can learn more about their life and work.

# PICTURE ACKNOWLEDGMENTS

Figures